ESSE

Iceland: Regions and Best places to see

Original by Ann F Stonehouse
Updated by Ann F Stonehouse

© Automobile Association Developments Limited 2007
First published 2007

ISBN-10: 0-7495-4956-4
ISBN-13: 978-0-7495-4956-5

Published by AA Publishing, a trading name of Automobile Association Developments
Limited, whose registered office is Fanum House, Basing View, Basingstoke,
Hampshire RG21 4EA.
Registered number 1878835.

Colour separation: MRM Graphics Ltd
Printed and bound in Italy by Printer Trento S.r.l.

A02694
Maps in this title produced from mapping © MAIRDUMONT / Falk Verlag 2005

About this book

Symbols are used to denote the following categories:

- ✚ map reference to maps on cover
- ✉ address or location
- ☎ telephone number
- ⏰ opening times
- ✋ admission charge
- 🍴 restaurant or café on premises or nearby
- 🚌 nearest bus/tram route
- ⛴ nearest ferry stop
- ✈ nearest airport
- ❓ other practical information
- ❗ tourist information office
- ➤ indicates the page where you will find a fuller description

The essence of Iceland pages 6–17
Introduction; Features; Food and Drink; Short Break including the 10 Essentials

Planning pages 18–31
Before You Go; Getting There; Getting Around; Being There

Best places to see pages 32–53
The highlights of any visit to Iceland

Best things to do pages 54–67
Good places to have lunch; top activities; Reykjavík nightlife and more

Exploring pages 68–156
The best places to visit in Iceland, organized by area

Maps
All map references are to the maps on the covers. For example, Reykjavík has the reference ✚ 18J – indicating the grid square in which it is to be found.

Prices
The cost of restaurants and cafés at attractions is given by £ signs:
£££ denotes higher prices, ££ denotes average prices, £ denotes lower prices.

Hotel prices
Prices are per room per night:
£ budget (under ISK6,000);
££ moderate (ISK6,000–9,000);
£££ expensive to luxury (over ISK9,000)

Restaurant prices
Two-course meal per person without drinks: £ budget (under ISK1,200);
££ moderate (ISK1,200–2,000);
£££ expensive (over ISK2,000)

Icelandic characters
In this book we have shown the Icelandic character ð as Ð/ð , pronounced as a hard 'th' as in 'then'. The Icelandic character Þ/þ, is pronounced as a soft 'th' as in 'thistle' (see also page 30).

Contents

BEST THINGS TO DO

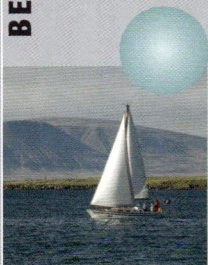

54 – 67

EXPLORING...

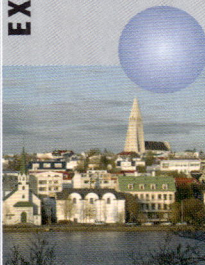

68 – 156

The essence of...

First-time visitors arriving at Keflavík airport look out on the surprisingly fresh-looking lunar landscape of Iceland and wonder what they've done. Most find themselves hooked and come back again and again.

features

At a mere 20 million years old, this is the youngest country in Europe, an island just bigger than Ireland (350km/217 miles from south to north, 540km/335 miles from west to east) and lying across the vast undersea split known as the Mid-Atlantic Ridge, where two of the great plates of the earth's surface are pulling apart. This makes Iceland one of the world's most volcanically active sites, but it offers much more than just a live geography lesson.

For a start, it's a great place for outdoor activities, including hiking, horse-back riding, fishing and adventure sports. It's also an important breeding place for many rare birds and is blessed with sparkling clean air, the 'midnight sun', endless summer days and mid-winter Northern Lights. The mountains, fjords, rivers and waterfalls provide sweeping landscapes and diverse flora.

The Icelanders themselves generally welcome visitors and are proud to show off their country. Despite a small population of only around 285,000, Icelanders read more books per capita than any other country, love the latest gadgets and fashions, and usually speak several languages, including English. A vibrant and unique music scene has emerged here, with bands such as Sigur Rós and Björk known worldwide. Icelanders work hard to achieve one of the highest standards of living in the world; according to the UN, it's the second best place to live in the world. Most Icelanders would disagree, and place it firmly first.

Facilities for visitors have improved in recent years, but costs are high as so much has to be imported. The changeable weather and many unmade roads are notorious, but they needn't stop you getting to most places, though the remote and rocky interior is only accessible in high summer.

Make sure you don't try to see everything in one visit – the ring road looks a temptingly short way to

get around, but if you don't stop and explore properly you'll have missed most of what Iceland really has to offer. And the rewards are fantastic.

ICELAND'S FAMOUS
LEIFUR EIRÍKSSON (FL. AD1000)

Eldest son of Icelandic Viking Erik the Red, 'Leif the Lucky' is widely credited with the earliest European discovery of North America. He set sail from Greenland around AD1000 and is believed to have made landings on Baffin Island and down the east coast to the tip of Newfoundland before returning safely with claims of a lush land of paradise.

SNORRI STURLUSON (1179–1241)

Snorri was a powerful chief, Lawspeaker at the Alþthing (parliament) and descendant of the Viking hero and skaldic poet Egill Skallagrímson. He wrote the great Icelandic *Prose Edda* (a recording of Norse mythology), *Heimskringla* (the history of Norwegian kings) and probably *Egil's Saga* as well.

HALLDÓR LAXNESS (1902–98)

Born in Reykjavík, Halldór Laxness had his first novel, *Child of Nature*, published when he was just 17. He went on to write prolifically and was awarded the Nobel Prize for Literature in 1955. His best-known novel is *Independent People* (1946), set in the early 20th century, giving a realistically grim insight into peasant farming in Iceland.

BJÖRK GUDMUNDSDÓTTIR (1966–)

Björk cut her first disc at the age of 11 and became a member of punk-funk band the Sugarcubes, hitting world stardom with their song *Birthday* in 1988. She's since become Iceland's most popular export in her own recording right, with an inimitable vocal style and a constant ability to shock.

food & drink

Of necessity Icelanders live around the coastline of their island and, since fishing supports some 70 per cent of the economy, it's not really surprising that fish features largely in their diet.

Haddock *(ýsa)* is the national favourite, fresh and boiled or fried lightly. Cod *(thorskur)* is largely exported but you may find delicacies such as cod chins on the menu – try them, they are rich and delicious. Catfish *(steinbítur)* and halibut *(lúða)* are also widely available, and pickled herring *(síld)* is often served at breakfast. You'll see fish drying on wooden racks along the coast; this used to be a staple food to see poor farmers through the winter but now it's something of a delicacy – called *harðfiskur*, it looks like shredded loofah and has a

mild, not unpleasant fish taste, eaten smeared with butter *(smjör)*. Try it at the market in Kolaportið (► 78–79) before you buy. Pickling fish in whey is a speciality, celebrated in the Thorrablót festival in February.

Shellfish are also excellent, notably the small lobster *(humar)*. For freshwater fish, try the salmon *(lax)*, trout *(silungur)* and Arctic char *(bleikja)*.

The most notorious Icelandic dish is carefully rotted shark flesh *(hákarl)* which, when swilled down with a shot of the spirit *brennivín*, is supposed to induce a rapid state of intoxication – try it if you dare.

Icelanders boast that their lamb, fed on good pasture, comes ready-seasoned and it's certainly very good. Roasted, it's a traditional Sunday lunch, but you'll also find it salted *(saltkjöt)* and, particularly around Christmas, smoked like ham *(hangikjöt)*. Singed sheep head is a less appealing traditional item, eaten hot or cold, and you can buy it ready-pressed and gelled *(sviðasulta)*.

If you are determined to try the unusual, some restaurants serve puffin, guillemot and even fulmar, and at certain times you'll also see their mottled eggs for sale. The Icelanders have been eating them for years without denting the population, so don't feel too bad about it.

A ready supply of fruit and vegetables came late to this remote island, but the wonders of geothermal power harnessed to greenhouses in centres such as Hveragerði (➤ 101) mean that much more is now available, if not cheap. Bananas are actually grown in Akureyri.

Small cinnamon biscuits *(kex)* can be bought by the bagfull in any supermarket – and look out for the tasty donut knot, *kleinur*. A sweet, dark rye-bread is cooked slowly in the hot lava *(rúgbrauð)*, and at Christmas fragile flat cakes of thinly rolled and cut pastry are deep-fried *(laufabrauð* – see them out of season in the Christmas shop at Akureyri). Rye pancakes *(flatbrauð)* and large sweet pancakes are also eaten.

The low-fat dairy product *skyr* is widely available. Somewhere between cream cheese and yogurt, it is good served with cream and sugar or fresh fruit, and it also makes an excellent basis for cheesecake. Milk labelling can be confusing — *nýmjólk* is the normal stuff, while *léttmjólk* is semi-skimmed, *undanrenna* is skimmed and *súrmjólk* like thin yogurt. And of course ice-cream *(ís)* is eaten everywhere.

short break

Everything about Iceland is fascinating but there are certain experiences which should not be missed. If you only have a short time to visit Iceland, here are some of the essentials:

- **Relax in a thermally heated 'hot-pot';** they don't come more comfortable than the Blue Lagoon (➤ 34–35) but local swimming pools have them too.
- **Take the lift** to the top of the Hallgrímskirkja tower for the best views over Reykjavík (➤ 40–41).
- **Visit a Reykjavík sculpture gallery** and get to know more about Icelandic art – there's public sculpture everywhere and it's more fun if you know what you're looking at.
- **Go for a ride** on an Icelandic horse and try the unique 'fifth gait' for yourself – it's a leisurely way to explore the countryside.

- **Treat yourself to a trip onto a glacier** by snow-scooter or snow-tractor. Vatnajökull is the biggest in Europe but there are plenty of other choices.

- **Get off the Hringvegur (ring road)** into the mountains and the interior – and if the bumpy state of the side roads puts you off, enjoy the advantages of an organized tour.
- **Watch puffins,** everybody's favourite sea bird.
- **Eat fish** – there's a great selection of top restaurants to choose from. Try Við Tjörnina in Reykjavík (► 115), or Viðeyjarstofan on Viðey for the best.
- **Talk to the locals** for real insights – Icelanders have a keen national identity and pride, and are usually pleased to tell you more about their country.
- **Explore a steaming geothermal area** to understand why Iceland is as it is.

Planning

Before You Go

WHEN TO GO

JAN	FEB	MAR	APR	MAY	JUN	JUL	AUG	SEP	OCT	NOV	DEC
0.5°C	-1°C	-1.4°C	4°C	6.6°C	10.1°C	11.1°C	11.3°C	8.3°C	2.9°C	2.2°C	1.2°C
33°F	30°F	29°F	39°F	44°F	50°F	52°F	52.3°F	47°F	37°F	36°F	34°F

🟠 High season   🔵 Low season

If you want to see all of Iceland, you should be aware that the roads across the remote volcanic interior are only open to vehicles in July and August. At this time the rest of Iceland is green and relatively balmy, with almost 24-hour daylight, but it can be windy and wet. The main tourist season extends through June and September. If you come in winter or spring, be prepared for shorter, grey days and driving snow, which can block minor roads and make any route hazardous – ask for snow tyres on your hire car, and always check road conditions ahead. Few attractions outside the capital are open in winter. The Northern Lights may be seen under still, clear conditions in autumn, and between November and February.

WHAT YOU NEED

● Required
○ Suggested
▲ Not required

Some countries require a passport to remain valid for a minimum period (usually at least six months) beyond the date of entry – contact their consulate or embassy or your travel agent for details.

	UK	Germany	USA	Netherlands	Spain
Passport (or National Identity Card where applicable)	●	●	●	●	●
Visa (regulations can change – check before you travel)	▲	▲	▲	▲	▲
Onward or Return Ticket	▲	▲	▲	▲	▲
Health Inoculations (tetanus and polio)	▲	▲	▲	▲	▲
Health Documentation (➤ 21, Health Advice)	▲	▲	▲	▲	▲
Travel Insurance	●	●	●	●	●
Driving Licence (national)	●	●	●	●	●
Car Insurance Certificate	●	●	●	●	●
Car Registration Document	●	●	●	●	●

ADVANCE PLANNING
TOURIST OFFICES AT HOME

In the UK: Iceland Air, 172 Tottenham Court Road, 3rd floor, London, W1T 7LY
☎ 020 7874 1000;
www.visiticeland.com

In the USA: Icelandic Tourist Board 655 Third Avenue, New York, NY 10017 ☎ 212/ 885 9700;
www.icelandtouristboard.com

In Germany: Iceländisches Fremdenverkehrsamt, City Centre, Frankfurter-str, 181, D-63263 Neu-Isenburg, Germany
☎ 06102 254484;
www.icetourist.de

HEALTH ADVICE

Doctors Visitors from the EU are entitled to reciprocal state medical care and should take a EHIC which covers basic treatment. Citizens from elsewhere will need medical insurance. Note that extra medical insurance will not necessarily cover you for all activities. There is a 24-hour emergency ward at The National Hospital, Fossvogur ☎ 525 1700, and 24-hour duty doctors may be contacted on ☎ 5251000.

Dental services Ask at your hotel or guest house for details of local English-speaking dentists. An emergency number for cover in Reykjavík is ☎ 575 0505.

TIME DIFFERENCES

| GMT 12 noon | Iceland 12 noon | Germany 1PM | USA (NY) 7AM | Netherlands 1PM | Spain 1PM |

Iceland is on GMT all year. It does not go on to daylight saving time. In the north of the island, the sun does not fully set June; correspondingly, in January there may be only 3.5 hours of daylight in that region.

WHAT'S ON WHEN

1 January *New Year:* Celebrations start the afternoon before – a great excuse for bonfires and fireworks.

6 January *Twelfth Night:* More bonfires and fireworks to brighten up the long dark nights.

Late January–late February
Þorrablót: Celebration of traditional winter foods. Delicacies such as whey-pickled fish and rams' testicles are washed down with brennivín.

April *Shrove Tuesday:*
'Bursting Day' (Sprengidalur) is commemorated by feasting on lamb and pea soup. The previous Monday is 'Bun Day' (Bolludagur), when children go round threatening to beat the grown-ups with sticks, and demanding buns.

Easter: Everything closes from Maundy Thursday to Easter Monday. On Ash Wednesday (Öskudagur), children attempt to hang little bags of ashes on the backs of unsuspecting adults.

Around 20 April *First Day of Summer (Sumardagurinn fyrsti):* An important landmark Thursday which is celebrated in laid-back carnival style.

Early June *Seamen's Day (Sjómannadagurinn):* Harbours are filled with ships and vessels of all sizes on this Sunday, and celebrations include rowing races and tugs of war.

17 June *National Day (Þjóðhátíð):* Carnival-type festivities are held all over Iceland.

Late June *The Arctic Open:* This cheerful four-day golf championship, open to professionals and amateurs, is played through the light summer nights on the world's most northerly golf course. At Akureyri, it lies 65° 40' north of the Equator.

International Viking Festival: Held every two years or so (last held in 2006), this is an unmissable Viking jamboree of singing, dancing, eating and fighting in the best traditions, held in Hafnarfjörður.

Early July *Höfn Lobster Festival (Hátíð á Höfn):* A big party with music, dance, competitions and feasting.

First weekend in August *Herring Festival (Síldarævintri):* Extensive celebrations in Siglufjorður, former herring capital of Iceland.

NATIONAL HOLIDAYS

JAN	FEB	MAR	APR	MAY	JUN	JUL	AUG	SEP	OCT	NOV	DEC
2		2	1	3	1	1	1	1	1	1	3

1 Jan	New Year's Day
April	Maundy Thursday, Good Friday, Easter Sunday, Easter Monday
April	First Day of Summer
1 May	Labour Day
May	Ascension Day
June	Whit Sunday
June	Whit Monday
17 June	National Day
Aug	Bank Holiday Monday
24 Dec	Christmas Eve
25 Dec	Christmas Day
26 Dec	Boxing Day
31 Dec	New Year's Eve

Most shops, offices and museums close on these days.

Early August *Westmann Islands Festival (Þjóðhátíð):* Independence Day party, held on Heimaey, with barbecues, bonfires and roistering.

September *Reltir:* Round-ups on horse-back are held all over the country, bringing sheep and horses down from the hills before winter sets in.

23 December *Þorláksmessa:* Celebrated in the best restaurants by the eating of cured skate.

24–25 December Christmas officially starts at noon on the 24th, and presents are exchanged on that day.

Yuletide Lads
Christmas for children in Iceland has its own special dimension. According to tradition, 13 boisterous 'Yuletide lads' come to call, one each night leading up to 25 December, to leave a small gift in the child's shoe placed in a window for that purpose. (If the child has been naughty, there'll be a potato in there in the morning instead.) The lads are pranksters and nicknamed accordingly – 'Sausage Snatcher', 'Door Slammer', 'Candle Snuffer' and so on. They are ruled over by a fearsome matriarch called Gryla, who eats bad children for breakfast. Her cat eats anyone without new clothes to wear on Christmas Day.

Getting There

ARRIVING

Iceland Express (**www.**icelandexpress.com) connects daily with London, Frankfurt and Copenhagen, and British Airways flies from London Gatwick (**www.**ba.com). Icelandair is the chief operator of international flights, flying from London, Glasgow, Copenhagen, Oslo, Paris, Stockholm, Amsterdam, Hamburg, Frankfurt, Zurich, Barcelona, Madrid, Milan, Boston, New York, Baltimore, Orlando, San Francisco and others. A regular shuttle bus operates between Keflavík airport and Reykjavík. Flybus bus transport to Keflavík airport from Icelandair Hótel Loftleiðir leaves about 2.5 hours before departure ☎ 562 1011.

FERRIES

The weekly car ferry from Denmark to Seyðisfjörður calls at Shetland, the Faroes and Norway. Contact Smyril Line Ísland, Sætúni 8, 101 Reykjavík, ☎ 570 8600; **www.**smyril-line.is.

CUSTOMS

YES Goods obtained duty-free. Limits:1L of spirits (up to 47% alcohol); 1L of wine (up to 21% alcohol) or 6L of beer; and 200 cigarettes or 250g of other tobacco products.

Up to three times the duty-free allowance for tobacco and alcohol may be brought into the country, subject to declaration at Customs and the payment of all additional Icelandic dues on them. You must be over 20 to benefit from alcohol allowances, and over 18 for the tobacco allowances.

Visitors are allowed to bring food into the country duty-free, for their own use in Iceland.

NO Uncooked vegetables, eggs, meat or dairy products; narcotics; firearms; unlicensed plants or animals.

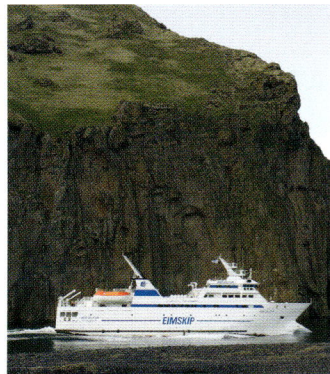

Getting Around

DRIVING
Drive on the right.

Speed limit on main tarmac roads:
90kph (56mph)
Speed limit on main gravel roads:
80kph (50mph)
Speed limit in populated areas:
30/50kph (19/31mph)

Seatbelts are mandatory in front and rear seats.

Icelandic law forbids driving after drinking alcohol, and the penalties are severe.

Unleaded petrol is available as 95 octane (regular) and 98 octane (super). Filling stations around Reykjavík are open daily 7.30am–8pm or later; around the country, times may vary, and some are open only in summer. Some filling stations have automats which take ISK500, ISK1000, ISK2000 notes and credit and debit cards after hours, but these do not always work. Petrol stations can be few and far between, so don't let your fuel run low.

In case of breakdown, telephone your hire car company or ☎ 5112

112 for emergency assistance. (The Icelandic motoring organization FIB has reciprocal agreements with AAA and European clubs like AA.)

CAR RENTAL
Car rental is expensive so shop for the best deal – you may be able to combine with a fly-drive or farm-stay package, for example. A 4WD is essential if you plan going far off the main roads, and spiked snow tyres for winter driving in snowy conditions. Check the cover – hire companies may not insure you on some routes.

**MOTORING INFORMATION
DRIVING CONDITIONS**
Most of Route 1 is now tarmac but other roads are often unsurfaced gravel. Be prepared to slow right down when passing other vehicles, as loose gravel can be thrown up and road edges are soft; be

cautious at narrow bridges and blind summits, and be prepared to give way (flashing headlights usually mean 'I'm coming through'). Stay on the roads and tracks. The natural environment is fragile and off-road driving carries heavy fines.

Headlights must be switched on at all times when driving, day and night. On roundabouts, cars on the inside lane have right of way.

DRIVING IN THE INTERIOR
Many roads across central Iceland are open for only a few weeks in high summer, as weather conditions can change very quickly. If you're planning a trip, consult tourist information and locals before you set out and be especially cautious at unbridged rivers.

ANIMALS
Note that sheep, horses and cattle may stray onto the roads and you are liable to pay compensation for any animal injured or killed. Farm dogs chasing cars can be a particular hazard.

ON THE ROAD
On your travels you may find that, with such a small and scattered resident population, there are long distances between towns with restaurants. The network of petrol stations comes to the rescue here, acting not only as essential toilet stops, but always with a pot of hot coffee on tap and usually offering a range of other snacks, including the ubiquitous hotdogs. And among the household-name chocolate bars, you'll discover liquorice in every conceivable form – very much a local favourite.

PUBLIC TRANSPORT
INTERNAL FLIGHTS
Flugfélag Íslands (Air Iceland ☎ 570 3030; **www.**airiceland.is) is the main operator of domestic flights and flights to the Faroes and Greenland, out of Reykjavík; Mýflug

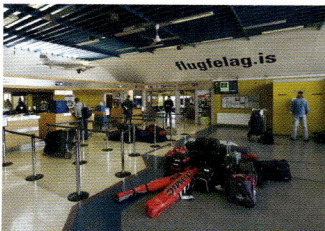

(☎ 464 4400) operates sightseeing flights from Mývatn. Íslandsflug has regular flights to the Westmann Islands ☎ 481 3300.

BUSES
Reykjavík's main BSÍ coach terminal is at Vatnsmýrarvegur 10 ☎ 552 2300. There are regular daily coach services around the country, even in winter. You can buy good value 'passport' tickets if you intend to travel widely on the network.

operate 7am–12pm Mon–Sat, and 10am–12pm Sun; some weekend buses run until 4am. The fare is standard ISK220 for adults (reduced for teenagers/children) and you need exact money for the ticket machine; alternatively, buy a book of tickets in advance and pay less. If you have to change buses on your journey, buy a *skiptimiða* (transfer ticket) from the driver, and you'll still pay only ISK220.

FERRIES
Local ferries operate between the mainland and islands or remote areas. There are more frequent services in summer.
Viðey ☎ 533 5055
Flatey ☎ 438 1450
Hrísey ☎ 466 1797/852 2211
Westmann Islands ☎ 481 2800

URBAN TRANSPORT
Reykjavík's yellow city buses operate from Hlemmur, at the eastern end of Laugavegur, or the central Lækjartorg square. They

TAXIS
Widely available, many offer personalized taxi tours at fixed prices.
Hreyfill ☎ 588 5522
Borgarbíll ☎ 552 2440
BSO (Akureyri) ☎ 461 1010
BSR ☎ 561 0000

Being There

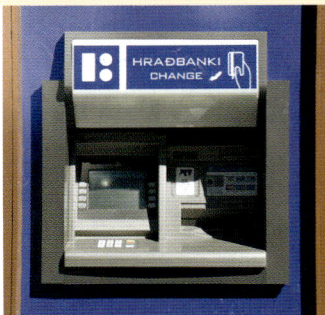

TOURIST OFFICE
Tourist Information Centre
✉ Aðalstræti 2, Reykjavík
☎ 590 1550 🕓 Jun–Aug, daily
8.30–6; Sep–May, Mon–Fri 9–1
and 2–5, Sat 10–2

CONSULATES
UK Laufásvegur 31,Reykjavík
☎ 550 5100
Germany Laufásvegur
31,Reykjavík ☎ 530 1100
USA Laufásvegur 21, Reykjavík
☎ 562 9100

CURRENCY AND FOREIGN EXCHANGE
Currency The monetary unit of
Iceland is the króna, plural krónur
(kr). The international abbreviation
is ISK. Notes are in denominations
of 500, 1000, 2000 and 5000, and
coins of 1, 5, 10, 50, 100.

Exchange Foreign currencies and
travellers' cheques can be
exchanged at all banks, savings
banks and bureaux de change.
Credit cards are widely accepted.

HEALTH AND SAFETY
Drugs Most pharmacies (Apótek)
have English-speaking staff. For
24-hour opening ☎ 118.

Safe water Cold tap water is some
of the cleanest and best in the
world (beware of the hot, which
may come from natural thermal
sources and smell faintly
sulphurous). In the hills, clean
spring water is usually safe to drink
but avoid glacial meltwater.

Petty crime Iceland is generally a
safe country with a low crime rate,
although petty crime is on the
increase. Leave money and
valuables in the hotel safe. Carry
only what you need and keep it out
of sight. On Friday and Saturday
nights in central Reykjavík, and
Akureyri, drunkenness can be a
nuisance, but the mood is usually
boisterous rather than violent.

TELEPHONES
Public telephones (sími) are usually
found outside the post office. They
take coins (ISK10, 50 and 100) or
phone-cards – available from post
offices/telephone stations.

OPENING HOURS

- ● Shops
- ● Offices
- ● Banks
- ● Attractions/Museums
- ● Post Offices
- ● Pharmacies

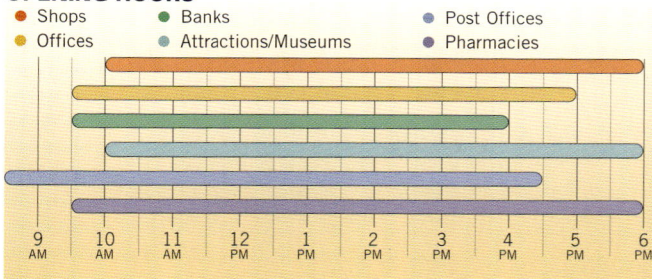

| 9 AM | 10 AM | 11 AM | 12 PM | 1 PM | 2 PM | 3 PM | 4 PM | 5 PM | 6 PM |

Most shops are open for a shorter time on Saturday, often closing at 4 or earlier, but may stay open until 7 on Fridays. Office hours may be earlier in summer. Banks may stay open for longer on Thursdays and Fridays. Money exchange services in Reykjavík are available at the Tourist Information Centre, Aðalstræti 2, Jun–Aug, daily 8.30–6; Sep–May, Mon–Fri 9–1 and 2–5, Sat 10–2.

EMERGENCY TELEPHONE NUMBERS

Police: 112
Fire: 112
Ambulance: 112

INTERNATIONAL DIALLING CODES

From Iceland to:
UK: 00 44
Germany: 00 49
USA and Canada: 00 1
Netherlands: 00 31

PATRONYMICS

The phone book is alphabetically organized by first names as people in Iceland, from the Prime Minister down, are widely called by their given first name. Children take their father's name as their surname, adding 'son' or 'daughter' at the end. For example, husband and wife Jón Arnarson and Svava Stefánsdóttir could have two children, a boy and a girl, Magnús Jónsson and Erla Jónsdóttir.

INTERNET

A growing number of cafés in Reykjavík offer Internet access. Try the Ráðhúskaffi in the town hall, by the Tjörn, or Kleif Travel Market on Bankastræti. The BSÍ bus terminal on Vatnsmýrarvegur and the main tourist office also have access.

POSTAL SERVICES

Post offices are found in the main settlements around Iceland, and opening hours are generally Mon–Fri 9–4.30. Stamps can also be bought in most souvenir outlets where postcards are sold. Icelandic stamps are particular interest for collectors.

ELECTRICITY

The power supply in Iceland is 220 volts, 50HZ. Sockets accept two-pin round plugs. UK visitors require a plug adaptor and US visitors will need a transformer for appliances operating on 100–120 volts.

WHEN DEPARTING

The Flybus link to Keflavík airport leaves from Hótel Loftleiðir and other main city centre hotels approximately 2.5 hours before each flight, ☎ 562 1011. Cost ISK1,150. Free pick-up can be arranged from major hotels and guesthouses in the city. You can also check in luggage in advance – contact the number above for details. Keep any details handy for tax refunds on major purchases.

TIPPING

There is no tradition of tipping in Iceland, and giving a tip may cause offence.

LANGUAGE

Icelandic is directly related to Old Norse and people with a knowledge of a Scandinavian language will therefore have a head start. For the rest of us, it's pretty impenetrable, but a limited guide to pronunciation will help the guesswork, especially when you are trying to find your way around the country.

Two unfamiliar letters are: Ð/ð, (or more properly ð) pronounced as a hard th, as in 'then' (for example, Herðubreið); and Þ/þ, which is pronounced as a soft, aspirated th, as in 'thistle' (for example, Þingvellir, prounouced Thingvellir).

The letter j is pronounced as a y (for example, Jökulsárlón). When f is found before an l or n (for example, Hafnarfjörður) it is pronounced as p. The letter h takes on a k-sound when in front of l, r or v (for example, Hlemmur).

When r is before l and n it takes on an extra d-sound (for example Perlan, which sounds like Perdlan). The double ll sounds rather like the Welsh equivalent, a soft 'kl' sound made somewhere in the back of the mouth (for example, Hellnar).

It's a relief to know that English is widely spoken, but even a few basic words of greeting will help to break down barriers.

Accommodation

hotel	*hótel*	guesthouse	*gistihús*
room	*herbergi*	toilet	*klósett/salerni*
single/	*fyrir einn/*	view	*útsýni*
double	*fyrir tvo*	campsite	*tjaldsvæði*

Money

bank	*banki*	credit card	*kreditkort*
exchange office	*exchange/banki*	traveller's cheque	*ferðatékki*
post office	*póstur*	passport	*vegabréf*
cash desk	*afgreiðsla*		

Food and drink

breakfast	*morgunverður*	wine/beer	*vín/bjór*
lunch	*hádegismatur*	coffee/tea	*kaffi/te*
dinner	*kvöldmatur*	water	*vatn*
restaurant	*veitingahús*	bread	*brauð*
café	*kaffihús*	fruit	*ávöxtur*
menu	*matseðill*	dessert	*eftirréttur*

Transport

aeroplane	*flugvél*	...port/harbour	*höfn*
airport	*flugvöllur*	ticket	*miði*
bus	*strætisvagn*	...single/return	*aðra leið/*
coach	*rúta*		*báðar leiðir*
...station	*stoppistöð/*	car	*bíll*
	strætisvagnastöð	taxi	*taxi*
...stop	*strætisvagnastopp*	no smoking	*ekki reykja*
boat	*bátur*	timetable	*tímatafla*

Conversation

yes/no	*já/nei*	my name is...	*ég heiti...*
please	*gerðu thað*	sorry	*fyrirgefið*
thank you	*takk*	excuse me	*fyrirgefið*
hello	*hæ*	help!	*hjálp!*
goodbye	*bless/bæ*	Sunday	*sunnudagur*
good morning	*góðan daginn*	Monday	*mánudagur*
good evening	*gótt kvöld*	Tuesday	*thriðjudagur*
I don't understand	*ég skil ekki alveg*	Wednesday	*miðvikudagur*
I don't speak	*ég tala ekki*	Thursday	*fimmtudagur*
Icelandic	*íslensku*	Friday	*föstudagur*
where is...?	*hvar er...?*	Saturday	*laugardagur*

Best places to see

1

Bláa Lóniđ (Blue Lagoon)

www.bluelagoon.is

A pool beside a power station in the middle of a windswept lava field sounds missable, but the famous Blue Lagoon is an absolute must.

In fact it's so good, you may want to go several times during your stay, as it's a great way to relax and unwind from all that sightseeing. The pool is actually geothermally heated seawater, rich in natural minerals, so you feel wonderfully buoyant as you float around in the silky warmth. It's the natural by-product of the nearby Svartsengi power station, usually tactfully hidden in clouds of steam, which uses water straight from 2,000m (6,560ft) below the ground which is at a much higher temperature. Once it has cooled down, the water is the comfortable temperature of a hot bath and you can simply lie back in the open air and think of Iceland – even if it's snowing on your head! The opacity comes from the natural white silica mud mixed with minerals and an algae, which gives it the trade-mark milky blue colour, whatever the weather. Buckets of soapy white gunge are placed around the margins – it's a pleasant sludge of the silica and minerals and you can smear it over yourself for glorious exfoliation. It's supposed to be good for skin conditions (there's a special pool dedicated to psoriasis sufferers, who find great relief) and you'll certainly come away with silky-feeling skin.

The bottom is comfortable sand and the water gets no deeper than adult shoulder-height, so non-swimmers can feel confident. However children under the age of 11 must be supervised. There's always a lifeguard on duty, just in case, fully clothed against the elements for it's much colder in the air than in the water. Book ahead for a spa massage, or simply stand under the waterfall for a natural, shoulder-pounding massage in the main pool.

✚ 17H ✉ 5km (3 miles) from Grindavík, off Route 43, 45 minutes southwest of Reykjavík ☎ 420 8800 🕔 All year, daily ✋ Moderate 🍴 Snack bar (£). Good restaurant caters for up to 350 (£–££) 🚌 Regular service from main bus station in Reykjavík, also calls in at bigger hotels on request ❓ You can hire swimsuits, bath robes and towels. Take shampoo ℹ Tourist Information, Icelandic Saltfish Museum, Hafnargötu 12a, Grindavík ☎ 420 1109

2 Flatey

This beautiful island in Breiðafjörður bay is one of the prettiest spots in Iceland and an unexpected secret makes it well worth the effort to get there.

Its name tells you there are no exciting natural features in store – Flatey simply means 'flat island' and as you walk up from the harbour there is nothing especially remarkable about the old wooden houses grouped there, gracious and appealing though they are. Take the well-trodden path that leads through the grassy meadowland, bursting with buttercups and patrolled by anxious Arctic terns, which nest on the ground here in large numbers. Look carefully and you may spot the downy grey chicks, but mind your head – the terns can peck you hard and sharp if they think you're getting too close.

This way leads to the wooden church, deceptively modest in its simple lines for the interior is like no other. Most Lutheran churches are free of embellishment but this one has been painted with a rich set of frescoes, depicting local folk in biblical settings. The effect is breathtaking. The brushstrokes are bold and black, the figures vivid and engaging – note a young, unmistakably Icelandic 'Christ the Fisherman' over the altar. The murals are the work of a Spanish–Icelandic painter, Baltasar, who came here in the 1960s and worked for his keep over a period of several years.

The church is not the only surprise on this extraordinary island. Tucked just behind it is a tiny wooden shed – peer through the murky windows and you'll recognize the smallest and oldest library in Iceland, a legacy of Flatey's historic importance as a trading and religious centre. One of the great medieval manuscripts, *Flateyjarbók*, was held here until its dispersal to Denmark – it's now in the Culture House in Reykjavík.

✚ 3C ✉ Middle of Breiðafjörður bay ☎ 438 1413
🍴 Small restaurant Veitingastofan Vogur (£–££), with limited accommodation, open summer only 🚢 Ferry Baldur from Stykkishólmur calls in daily ☎ 438 1450;
www.seatours.is ❓ Look out for white-tailed sea-eagles around the islands of Breiðafjörður
ℹ Tourist Information Centre, Borgarbraut, Stykkishólmur
☎ 438 1450

3 Gullfoss and Geysir

Two of Iceland's most spectacular and famous natural sights are found within a few kilometres of each other near the head of a great valley.

Gullfoss is the 'golden waterfall' on the River Hvítá, the most outstandingly beautiful in this land of tumbling water. You can usually see the cloud of vapour and hear the roar long before you see it, set sideways on at the top of a long, narrow gorge which reaches depths of 70m (230ft). It is in fact two falls, one immediately above the other and at right angles to it, so you get double the effect. You can view the falls from the railed-off point above or take the path that leads right down to the water, but be warned – you're liable to get wet just from the spray there!

It's hard to imagine anybody wanting to destroy this wonder of nature, but in 1907 it came under threat from developers who sought to contain it for hydroelectric power. They were opposed by a young woman, Sigríður Tómasdóttir, from the neighbouring farm of Brattholt, and her campaign to save the waterfall and its gorge was ultimately successful. She's known as the heroine of the falls and her statue stands by the visitor centre.

In contrast, the spouting steam vents on the hillside at Geysir (pronounced 'gayzeer') have been valued since their first appearance in the 13th century, but alas, the original great Geysir, which gave its name to the phenomenon, no longer blows. It was probably blocked over the centuries by eager sightseers, who threw any handy debris into the bubbling pool to accelerate the spouting. More recent moves to replumb it have damaged it beyond repair. However, Geysir's smaller neighbour Strokkur is well worth seeing in its own right, and goes off every ten minutes or so, shooting boiling steam some 30m (114ft) into the air (make sure you stand up-wind). It's fascinating to watch as the water in the circular pool at its base is sucked in and out by the pressure of hot geothermal water and cold river water down below, as though you were standing on the back of a living being rather than stone. When the pool is almost full, the water at the centre suddenly bubbles up in a luminous blue swell and the plume of steam erupts with a great hiss – not to be missed.

✚ 20K ✉ 125km (78 miles) east of Reykjavík, on Route 35 🕐 Open access ✋ Free; small charge for multimedia presentation at visitor centre 🍴 Hotels, restaurant and coffee shop at Geysir; café at Gullfoss 🚌 Both sites, classic Golden Circle coach tours, half day or whole day ℹ️ Geyser Centre ☎ 486 8915; www.geysisstofa

4 Hallgrímskirkja, Reykjavík

www.hallgrimskirkja.is

Like a giant space shuttle about to take off, the dramatic white tower of the Hallgrímskirkja looms over the old town district of Reykjavík.

Completed in 1974, the church took some 30 years to build, and locals are still getting used to it, but – love it or hate it – you won't get far away from it, for it seems to watch you down every street. It's the most striking modern building in Iceland, was designed by Guðjón Samúelsson (1887–1950), and is named after the 17th-century hymn-writer and poet Reverend Hallgrímur Pétursson. It actually stands at the top of Skólavörðustígur and, by the time you have panted your way up the hill, you'll find this a breathtaking building in more senses than one.

While rockets come to mind when you see the church from a distance, close-up its concrete pillars resemble giant hexagonal volcanic columns, or even a fantastical set of organ pipes. Step through the door and it is like being inside a towering ice-cathedral, very cool and unadorned, grey and white, with narrow gothic windows of clear glass showing strips of sky. Turn around and you'll see the huge organ, vulgar by comparison – it boasts 5,275 steely pipes, each sponsored by members of the congregation. The simple furnishings you might

expect of a Lutheran church here become minimalist and very stylish. They include a font of clear rock crystal, made in the Czech Republic, and mounted on a block of Icelandic rock. You can take the lift to the 8th floor of the tower, 73m (239ft) high, for a panorama over the rooftops of Reykjavík. The heroic statue in front of the Hallgrímskirkja is of Leifur Eiríksson, credited with the first European discovery of America around AD1000.

✚ *Reykjavík 4c* ✉ Skólavörðuholt ☎ 510 1000 🕐 Church May–Sep daily 9–6; Oct–Apr daily 9–5. Tower daily 10–5 ✋ Tower cheap 🚌 7 ❓ Service Sun 11am. Regular organ recitals Jul and Aug, Thu 12
ℹ️ Tourist Information Centre, Aðalstræti 2 ☎ 590 1550

5 Jökulsárgljúfur

The narrow strip of Jökulsárgljúfur encompasses a magnificent valley, a deep gorge, mysterious echoing rocks and Europe's most powerful waterfall.

The park follows the canyon formed by the Jökulsá á Fjöllum, one of the major rivers which churns northwards from Vatnajökull (▶ 155). It is believed the canyon was originally formed in the course of a few days, following an explosion of the volcano and subsequent release of meltwater *(jökulhlaup)*.

    At the park's southern end is Dettifoss, a massive waterfall 45m (171ft) high and 100m (328ft) wide, over which the river pours at an incredible rate. It's glacial meltwater, so it's filthy –

this is not a pretty waterfall but its power is awesome. You can hear the roar some distance away and when you stand next to it the effect is shattering to the senses (be careful, there are no barriers). There's a footpath down the western side, back to Ásbyrgi, which takes two days to complete, and as you work your way downstream you'll see smaller falls at Hafragilsfoss and Selfoss. There are plenty of short walks in the area – information is available from the ranger stations at Ásbyrgi and Vesturdalur.

The half-way point of the canyon is Hólmatungur, lush and green and full of wild flowers in summer. Further north, the strange craggy rocks of Hljóðaklettar, near the Vesturdalur campsite, are famous for their echoes. The northern end of the park at Ásbyrgi is also its most accessible point. Here the canyon opens into a beautiful wide horseshoe-shaped valley, reputedly a hoofprint left behind by the god Odin's horse Sleipnir. The high walls protect a basin full of birch and rowan trees, with an outcrop, Eyjan, floating in the middle, a perfect island in a sea of green.

✚ 12D ✉ Main entrance from Kelduhverfið, west of Ásbyrgi ☎ 465 2195 (National Park information)
🌐 Access is limited by the state of the roads, open only in summer ✋ Free 🍴 Café at Ásbyrgi petrol station
❓ Access roads to west (F862) and east (864). Keep to west for Hljóðaklettar, but road deteriorates to jeep track south of Dettifoss
ℹ Tourist Information Centre, Hafnarstræti 82, Akureyri
☎ 462 7733; www.eyjafjordur.is

6 Jökulsárlón

www.jokulsarlon.is

Icebergs of extraordinary age and beauty float on this glacial lagoon, separated from the sea by only a narrow slip of land.

After the monotony of the surrounding landscape and the coal-black of the *sandur* (glacial gravel) shore, the luminous beauty of the icebergs at Jökulsárlón always surprises. Even on a grey day the compressed ancient turquoise ice, humbug-striped with black glacial morraine, seems to be lit from within as the bergs move in a stately slow dance in the wind. The little that shows on the surface can seem as big as a house, and the view shifts subtly from hour to hour. They are calves of

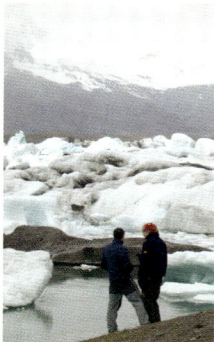

the great Breiðamerjkur glacier which looms up behind, its snout stained black with lava grit. It has been flowing down these mountains for centuries and, as photos in the little café show, it has grown and retreated over the years, gouging a lake 100m (320ft) deep with icy waters that pour through into the sea. It is in danger of breaking through altogether one day, sweeping Route 1 and the fragile suspension bridge with it.

There are good points for photography on both sides of the bridge, and it's worth taking the amphibious vehicle tour down into the lake to get close amongst the icebergs. You can often see seals fishing in the swift channel, eider ducks swim fearlessly between the shifting ice blocks, and in summer the air is electric with the sharp cries and territorial posturing of Arctic terns. If the tour buses spoil your view, then Breiðarlón is another iceberg lagoon to the south, easily accessed on foot from the main road.

✚ 26J ✉ Just off Route 1, 75km (47 miles) west of Höfn 🕐 Open access ✋ Free 🍽 Small visitor centre and café on site, open in summer from mid-May 🚤 Amphibious vehicle trips leave at regular intervals for a tour of the lake ℹ Tourist Information Centre, Litabrú 2, Höfn ☎ 478 1500

7 Mývatn

Birds in their thousands come to nest in this conservation area of water and greenery set in an active geothermal area.

It is said that more duck species breed here than anywhere else in the world, 15 in total, including the colourful harlequin, Barrow's goldeneye, scaup, tufted and long-tailed ducks. You'll also find whooper swans, Slavonian grebes and both red-throated and great northern divers. Their breeding ground is mostly to the west of the lake and this area is closed to traffic in high summer.

The birds are part of an ecosystem based on the millions of midges and flies which give the lake its name (pronounced meevatn) and also provide food for salmon and char. Their microscopic skeletons have gathered on the lake bottom and support a different economy – diatomite processing in a factory east of Reykjahlið, for use in industrial filters, fertiliser and paint.

The lake averages a depth of only 2.5m (9.5ft) and covers some 37sq km (14 sq miles). It's in a shallow depression and is full of small green islands. These include many 'pseudo-craters' – looking like mini-volcanoes, they are actually the result of gas-explosions under the lava. Extensive

areas show where the rock crust has been cracked by upheavals below, and lava has bubbled up and petrified under the water.

Námafjall is an extraordinary sulphurous hillside to the east, streaked with red and yellow, with grey boiling mud pools and steam-vents an overwhelming vision of Hell. Exploratory activity at the nearby geothermal power station, Krafla, is believed to have set off more earthquakes. Mývatn has its own 'Blue Lagoon', the **Nature Baths,** offering summer bathing until midnight.

➕ 12C ✉ 99km (61 miles) east of Akureyri 🕑 Open access 🍴 Several cafés and restaurants around Reykjahlið (£–£££) ❓ The midges can get in your nose, ears, mouth and hair, so a netted hat is recommended for Jun and Aug. Hire a bicycle for leisurely exploration ☎ 464 4220
ℹ Tourist Information Centre in Strax supermarket
☎ 464 4390
Nature Baths
☎ 464 4411; www.naturebaths.com

8 Skaftafell

Approaching Skaftafell National Park from the west, a panorama of green hills, tumbling ice and gothic mountain pinnacles fills your view.

As you get closer, the scene resolves into three deeply crevassed glaciers, with Skaftafellsjökull flanked by Morsárjökull to the left and Svínafellsjökull to the right, and a fourth, Skeiðarárjökull, much broader and flatter in appearance, over to your left. They are tributaries of the great ice-caps of Vatnajökull and Öræfajökull. You can follow the path up to the snout of Skaftafellsjökull, which pours down into a scenic lake surrounded by surprisingly lush vegetation, but be careful near the glacier where slippery clay overlays the ice under foot. If you want to walk on the glacier itself, make use of the expert ranger service which offers properly guided excursions, hikes and rock climbing.

Sheltered by the mountains, this site gets more than its fair share of good weather but can

also catch the rain. The campsite is a very popular place at weekends and so you may prefer to dodge the crowds and come mid-week. In summer the rounded hill behind the visitor centre, Skorar, is covered in birch woods and heath, and there are beautiful walks to the dramatic waterfall of Svartifoss (see walk ➤ 60) and into the next valley and the mountains behind. The woods are full of twittering redwings. Keep an eye open too for Iceland's smallest bird, a wren *(troglodytes islandicus)*, slightly larger than its mainland European cousin.

The braided gravel plain below Skaftafell was the scene of a massive *jökulhlaup* in 1996, when the volcano Grímsvötn erupted beneath Vatnajökull and the resulting flood waters swept away roads and bridges. Trucks and diggers, toy-sized in this vast landscape, constantly shift the gravel around in attempts to limit future damage.

🔲 25J ✉ 327km (203 miles) east of Reykjavík 🕐 Open access 🍴 Café at visitor centre (£) ✋ Free ❓ Mountain guide service ☎ 478 1627/894 2959
ℹ Visitor Centre 🕐 May–Sep ☎ 478 1627

9 Þingvellir

www.thingvellir.is

Iceland formed the first parliamentary democracy in the world at Þingvellir (Thingvellir), setting a system of government that would last for centuries.

The great fault line at Þingvellir, where the geological plates of America and Europe are tearing slowly apart, provided a remarkable natural arena for the gatherings of freemen, cheiftans and bishops to discuss matters of law and justice, crime and punishment. The first Alþing, or

parliament, was held here in AD930 and they continued annually (with some breaks) until 1789, when the plain fell 1m (3ft) in an earthquake and the power base shifted to Reykjavík. The Lawspeaker recited from memory one third of the country's laws each time. You can stand at his rock, marked with a flagpole and wooden platform, and survey the plain below where men would have gathered in temporary turf booths for two weeks each summer for the social event of the year. Sound echoes off the long line of sheer cliffs behind, making for excellent accoustics. Birch and willow grow amid the fissured rocks of the plain, with the lake to the south and low mountains in the distance, and the eye is drawn to the 19th-century church and the white-gabled farmhouse beside it. The classic view of the site is from the hill above and to the west, just off Route 36. By the approach to the church, one of the fissures of cold, clear water has become an oracle, with coins gleaming like fishscales at the bottom – ask your question as your coin falls and, if you can see it land on the bottom, the answer is 'yes'.

✚ 19J ✉ 49km (30 miles) northeast of Reykjavík on Route 361 🕐 Open access ✋ Free 🍴 Café (£) at visitor centre 🚤 Summer boat trips and fishing on the lake, book at visitor centre ❓ Good walk along chasm from Hótel Valhöll, past Lawspeaker's rock and the drowning pool Drekkingarhylor to Öxarárfoss waterfall
ℹ Visitor Centre for National Park, junction of routes 36 and 361 ☎ 482 2660/3606

10 Vestmannaeyjar (Westmann Islands)

www.vestmannaeyjar.is

This intriguing archipelago off the southwest coast includes Surtsey, a new island, and Heimaey, which suffered a devastating eruption in 1973.

The low black wedge of Surtsey emerged from the sea in a spew of flames and ash during the period 1963–6, the result of a submarine volcano on the same great faultline which is splitting the mainland. The island is protected so that scientists may study the growth and colonization of an island which reflects the creation of Iceland itself. Already small plants have taken root and even the first earthworm has been found.

Despite their settled appearance, none of the Westmann Islands is older than 5–10,000 years (infantile in geological terms) and parts of the biggest and only inhabited island, Heimaey (pronounced haymay), are a lot newer than that. The eruption of the volcano here on 23 January 1973 took everybody by surprise. By great luck, the fishing fleet was in and so the population of 5,000 was evacuated safely that same night. Then began an epic battle to prevent the town being totally destroyed by lava, which continued to flow for five months; seawater was pumped over it and you can see clearly how the flow stopped just short of the harbour. In fact, the new rock narrowed the harbour mouth to make it one of the safest anchorages in Iceland.

The gritty lava on Eldfell is still warm to the touch, and hot enough below the surface to bake bread – you can climb it for a great view over the town and of the green amphitheatre of Herjólfsdalur, where locals have their own three-day mega-party in early August. Look out for puffin hunters on the cliffs opposite the harbour. Their selective catch makes little dent on the population.

✚ 20G ✉ 11km (7 miles) off south coast 🍴 Various places on Heimaey (£–£££) ⛴ Ferry from Þorlákshöfn takes 3 hours ☎ 481 2800 ✈ Flights from Reykjavík and Selfoss to Heimaey; also sightseeing flights over Surtsey
ℹ Tourist Information Centre, Básaskersbryggja (ferry terminal), Heimaey ☎ 481 3555/2694

Best things to do

Good places to have lunch

Bautinn (£–££)
Unfussy, with the best hamburgers in town.
✉ Hafnarstræti 92, Akureyri ☎ 462 1818

Blaa Kannan (£)
Lunch in stylish surroundings – and leave room for cake.
✉ Strandgata 7, Akureyr ☎ 461 3999

Café Paris (£)
Bag a window seat, or dine al fresco if the sun's shining.
✉ Austervöllur, Reykjavík ☎ 551 1020

Café Sólon (£)
Great for a mid-shopping snack.
✉ Bankastræti 7A, Reykjavík ☎ 562 3232

Deli (£)
Freshly made baguettes, panini and salads for a quick, tasty lunch.
✉ Bankasæti 14, Reykjavík ☎ 551 6000

Fylgifiskar (£–££)
There are just a few tables in this fabulous fish shop, open
Monday to Friday (Saturday in winter).
✉ Suðurlandsbraut 10, Rekjavík ☎ 533 1303

Gamli Baukur (£–££)
Set right on the harbour, where it's all happening.
✉ Húsavík ☎ 464 2442

Kaffi Horniđ (£–££)
Simple food, well cooked.
✉ Hafnarbraut, Höfn ☎ 478 2600

Sufistinn Bókakaffi (£–££)
Relax with a coffee and a gâteau or savory snack in this peaceful
café above a bookshop.
✉ Laugavegur 18, Reykjavík ☎ 552 3740

Svarta Kaffiđ (£–££)
The home-made soup in a bread roll is a special winter warmer.
✉ Laugavegur 54, Reykjavík ☎ 551 2999

Top activities

Aerial sightseeing For a bird's-eye view of volcanoes and glaciers, Eagle Air (Flugfélagið Ernir) offer sightseeing flights from the airport in Reykjavík. The clear air means visibility can be pin-sharp, giving a great overview of the country. **Eagle Air** ☎ 562 4200

Birdwatching The concentration of nesting birds in Iceland makes it a paradise for birdwatchers. The main season for migrants is mid-May to mid-Aug, and two of the best places to see them are Mývatn and Látrabjarg (► 46–47, 103). If you're serious, try specialist tour operator **Naturetrek** ✉ Cheriton Mill, Cheriton, Alresford, Hampshire, UK, SO24 0NG ☎ 01962 733051; www.naturetrek.co.uk

Cycling Cycling around Iceland can be a bit of a challenge, with bumpy and unmade roads, and unpredictable weather. Sandstorms can be a hazard in the south. Still, people like to do it. Contact local tourist offices for information about cycle hire, and if you bring your own, bring plenty of spares. **Cycle paths** around Reykjvík: www.rvk.is/paths

Dolphin- and whale-spotting Several sites around Iceland offer facilities for this, and Húsavík is probably the best, but similar trips are offered from Reykjavík and other coastal settlements. **Norður-Sigling** ☎ 464 2350; www.nordursigling.is; **Gentle Giants** ☎ 464 1500; www.gentlegiants.is

Fishing With over 100 salmon rivers, 20 of them world-ranked, Iceland offers great sport fishing from mid-June to mid-September; but the best places are not cheap. Contact local tourist offices about opportunities and permits. **Reykjavík Tourist Information Centre** (► 28)

Hiking There's good local information and mapping to help you plan hiking routes in Iceland. The terrain, particularly in the interior, can be harsh, and weather conditions change very quickly, so seek expert advice on the correct equipment depending on your route and time of travel. The land is fragile, so camping outside official sites is discouraged, but there are over 100 campsites to choose from. See local tourist offices for listings.

Horse-riding Icelandic horses are small, surefooted and very comfortable to ride. The 'fifth gait' with head held high, unique to these horses, is much smoother than a bumpy trot and not as fast as a rollicking canter. Treks can be arranged to suit any ability and get you out into the wilds. **Ishestar Riding Tours** ☎ 555 7000; www.ishestar.is. **Skipalækur** by Egilsstaðir ☎ 471 1324

Swimming A ready supply of cheap hot water means that Iceland boasts more outdoor public swimming pools per head than the rest of Europe put together. The standard is high, entry prices low and there are often bubbling 'hot-pots' and water-chutes. Akureyri boasts one of the finest, but you'll find them in just about every town and settlement, often open until 8 or 9pm.

Winter sports There's not enough good snow for a lot of top-class skiing in Iceland, but the best is found in the north around Akureyri (**www.hlidarfjall.is**), which also has a new skating rink. Skidoos offer transport over the snowcaps all year round and trips are available around all the main glaciers. The snowmobiles are easy to operate and fun, if rather noisy and smelly, and can get you high into the wilds quickly – but stick close to your guide as there is a real danger of crevasses, especially in the summer. For advice on the best packages, contact Reykjavík tourist office (► 28).

a walk
around Skaftafell

Two walks lead from the visitor centre: a short one to the glacier, and this longer one to the waterfall of Svartifoss.

Walk towards the campsite, and bear right along the gravel path. Take the signed path to Svartifoss up hill, zigzagging through low birch and willow. Keep on the main path, cross a wooden bridge and climb the side of the gorge to reach the high Hundarfoss waterfall. Where the path branches keep right up the slope.

There are good views behind you over the plain, with rivers braiding across the gravel towards the sea. You can also see the broad snout of Skeiðarárjökull to the east.

Pass the smaller waterfall, Magnúsarfoss, and keep right, following signs for Svartifoss. Continue across an open area of moss, heather and crowberries.

Svartifoss, down to your left, appears as a dramatic black gash in the hillside. Columnar basalt forms an echoing natural amphitheatre of hanging columns, like organ pipes, surrounding the central water plume. The pointed mountain ahead is Skarðatindur, 1,385m (4,543ft).

Follow the precipitous path, which can be slippery, down to falls.

Enjoy a drink of the clear water and picnic on the rocks.

Scramble over the stepping stones and climb the rocky path – red-paint markers show the way. Turn up the steep hill, signed to Kristianartinder.

It's worth the long haul up for the views of the mountains from the viewing table.

Head back down hill, past the finger post, following signs to Lambhagi. Continue downhill and keep left a fork. Soon bear left, signed Lambhagi. Turn left and cross the stream above Magnúsarfoss. Retrace your steps down the main path back to the visitor centre.

Distance 4km (2.5 miles)
Time Allow two hours, longer with a picnic stop
Start/end point A circular walk; start from the National Park Visitor Centre ✚ 25J
Lunch Take a picnic to eat at the falls

Places to take the children

Hafnarfjörður

Rapidly developing as the Viking capital of Iceland, Hafnarfjörður boasts not only a fantastic Viking restaurant on the harbour front, including some life-sized models outside and a fascinating interior, but also an entire Viking 'village', where craftsmen can be seen at work in the West Nordic Cultural House (► 93).

Hafnarfjörður is also known as the Icelandic home of elves, who are thought to live in the rocks here. There are popular guided walks around the elf settlements of the town.

Information and bookings ☎ 694 2785; www.alfar.is

Hvalamiðstöðin (Whale Centre), Húsavík

This is a great place for children hoping to see whales and dolphins, with good pictorial information to identify the main species, real whale-skeletons so you get an idea of their size, and an amazing 'touch table' where you can compare the feel of whale-skin and shark-skin. There is a section dedicated to Keiko, killer-whale star of the film *Free Willy*, including a life-size model.

✉ Hafnarstétt ☎ 464 2520

Reykjavík Family Park and Zoo

This is a lively summer theme park and play area on a Viking theme, with an informal zoo including local species such as Icelandic horses, Arctic foxes and reindeer. Various activities for older kids include electric cars and diggers. Café, toilets and changing facilities on site. There's also a great swimming pool close by.

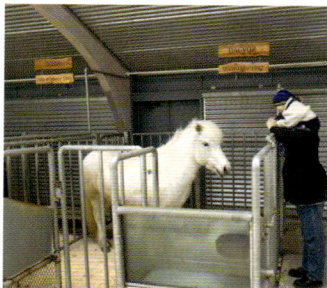

✉ Laugardalur park ☎ 575 7800; www.mu.is ✋ Inexpensive; free with City Tourist Card

Safnasafnið, Akureyri

The Icelandic Folk Art Museum lies 12km (7 miles) north of Akureyri, and contains a collection of colourful folk art pieces, from wooden cats to characterful dolls, toys and unusual sculpture.

✉ Svalbarðsströnd ☎ 461 4066 🕙 May to mid-Aug

The Sandgerði Nature Centre, Sandgerði

This popular centre on the western tip of Reykjanes promises 'instruction, exhibits, fun and adventure on land and sea', with everything from sailing to storytelling.

✉ Garðvegur 1 ☎ 423 7551/897 8007; www.sandgerdi.is
🕙 Daily ✋ Inexpensive

The Volcano Show, Reykjavík

Daily film shows of erupting volcanoes and earthquakes make a great introduction to the geology and landscape of Iceland. Films are held year round in the Red Rock Cinema, in several languages.

✉ Hellsundi 6a ☎ 845 9548

Reykjavík nightlife

In Reykjavík and other main centres, innocent cafés by day turn into pubs and clubs at night. The capital has a reputation for the quality and variety of night-time entertainment on offer. Friday and Saturday are the big nights, but don't start to get going until 11pm.

Broadway
Just out of the town centre, this disco in Hótel Ísland is said to be the biggest in Iceland. Live music and cabaret. Dress code.
✉ Ármúli 9 ☎ 533 1100; www.broadway.is

Café Romance Piano Bar
Intimate piano bar on the first floor of one of Reykjavik's oldest houses.
✉ Hafnarstræti 7 ☎ 562 4045

The Dubliner
Every city has an Irish theme pub, and Reykjavík is no exception. Locals say it was imported from the Emerald Isle (complete with staff) on the back of a lorry.
✉ Hafnarstræti 4 ☎ 511 3233

Gaukur á Stöng
The oldest pub in town, offering live music most evenings.
✉ Tryggvagata 22 ☎ 551 1556

Glaumbar
A sporty bar near the old harbour that likes to turn the music up.
✉ Tryggvagata 22 ☎ 552 6868

Hverfisbarinn
Located at the National Theatre, this is a café by day and lively bar in the evening.
✉ Hverfisgata 20 ☎ 511 6700

Kaffi Reykjavík

A good pub atmosphere in a large old building near the harbour. Dancing and live music at weekends.

✉ Vesturgata 2 ☎ 551 7759

Kaffibarinn

A trendy spot for posers and wannabes. Between the Hallgrímskirkja and the Tjörn.

✉ Bergstaðastræti1 ☎ 551 1588

Nasa

Bills itself as the biggest nightclub in the centre of the capital, popular with all ages.

✉ Austurvöllur ☎ 511 1313; www.nasa.is

Pravda

Nightclub and bar with trendy DJs and live bands, set in a former police station.

✉ Austurstræti 22 ☎ 552 9222

Sirkus

Ever-popular pub and nightclub, just off Laugavegur, with alternative music.

✉ Klapparstígur 31 ☎ 511 8022

Skuggabarinn

In the smart Hótel Borg, this is where the well-dressed dance the night away.

✉ Pósthusstræti 11 ☎ 551 1440

Sólon

Restaurant and gallery by day, bar by night, where the arty crowd hang out.

✉ Bankastræti 7a ☎ 562 3232; www.solon.is

Places to shop

Reykjavík Laugavegur is Reykjavík's famous shopping street, with lots of high-class designer fashion, hand-crafted jewellery, two great book stores (with books and magazines in all languages, not just Icelandic), and small cafés. Several shops cater exclusively for babies and toddler fashion – cute, but not cheap. For grown-up fashion, Pelsinn, beside the Domkirkjan, has a stylish range. More exclusive designer clothes, jewellery, and art and antiques shops are found on Skólavörðustígur.

Elsewhere, for Icelandic crafts try the Rammagerðin gift shop on Laugarvegur and Hafnarstræti, which stocks treasures from designer glassware to handmade wooden toys; the Traveller Shop on Bankastræti for maps, guides and novelties; and for gifts, jewellery and top-class woollens, historic Thorvaldsens Bazar (on the corner of Aðalstræti and Austurstræti) has a great selection – shop profits have supported children's charities for years. 12 Tonár, on Skólavörðustígur, is the place for Icelandic music, from Hjálmar and Sigur Rós to Hallbjörn Hjartarson, the 'Icelandic singing cowboy'. For top value, Álafoss, north of town in Mosfellsbær, is a factory outlet with woollens and other high-quality souvenirs.

Kringlan is the city's showpiece shopping mall, with more than 150 outlets – you can buy anything here from classy Swedish homeware to modern art. It's set away from the town centre but with a free car park underneath, and easy bus access. Find the latest fashions in Noa Noa, Boss, and the department store Hagkaup. For outdoor and camping gear you won't beat the vast Nanoq store, complete with artificial stream and climbing wall. Íslandia sells a wides range of souvenirs, from knitwear to lava candle-holders. The upper floor has a choice of fast food outlets, including a Hard Rock Café. The Smáralind shopping mall in Kópavogur includes some good boutiques among its more ordinary shops and international names such as Debenhams and Benetton.

If you want to take some Icelandic delicacies home with you, try the little market in Kolaportið, on Tryggvagata – it has everything from pancakes to great sides of smoked salmon, and you can often taste before you buy.

Akureyri also offers good shopping, though on a smaller scale. The main shopping street is pedestrianized Hafnarstræti, with the famous Bókval book and audio store on the corner. Fold-Anna is a factory outlet for beautiful woollen goods, including capes, blankets and hats. Listfléttan stocks some unusual and quality ceramics and art prints. Amarohúsið is a wide-ranging department store. For souvenirs, the Viking shop has a good range, and Gallerí Grúska, on Strandgata, is staffed by and for local artisans, with unusual handmade items such as fish-skin jewellery and eccentric hats. High fashion is found along Skipagata, with trendy designer outlets such as Perfect. Gleratorg is the town's shopping mall.

Tax-free shopping Visitors are entitled to reclaim 15 per cent on purchases of more than ISK4000 made at any shop displaying the 'tax-free' symbol. You pay the full price at the checkout, but ask and you'll be given a form to fill in. Hand this in at the airport bank when you leave showing the goods as proof, to obtain your refund – the saving is well worth it. You do not have to show woollen goods in this way. FOREX Bank, at Bankastræti 2, and The Centre, at Aðalstræti 2, can also refund tax for you.

Christmas every day Don't miss Jólagarðurinn, the red-painted house where it's Christmas every day, just out beyond Kjarnaskógar – stuffed with beautiful Christmas items, including traditional Icelandic decorations. You can picnic in the garden, alongside a whimsical wishing tree and fairytale tower.

Exploring

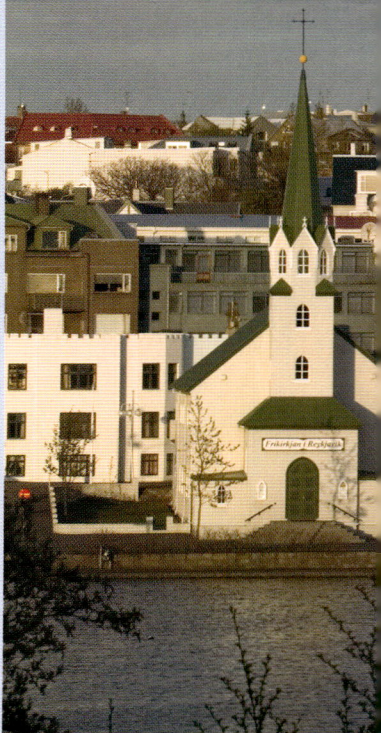

Iceland lies just below the Arctic Circle, and is a relatively new country, both in geological terms and habitation. Settlers arrived here from Norway only toward the end of the first century, and natural disasters, including volcanic eruptions, climate change, plague and trade embargoes all played a part in keeping the population low. Today some 293,000 people live here (60 per cent in the greater Reykjavík area, with Akureyri the only other city of any size) and in the last hundred or so years, their prosperity has increased dramatically. Most Icelanders enjoy a high standard of living, often holding down several jobs in order to maintain this. Nevertheless, there's a relaxed attitude to life, with little crime. The Icelandic language is related to Old Norse, proudly maintained in the face of globalization, and largely impenetrable to non-Scandinavians. English and Danish are also widely spoken.

Reykjavík and the West

This area encompasses a little of just about eveything Iceland has to offer.

The west of Iceland stretches from the majestic Snæfellsnes mountain ridge and the flatter lava-flow of the Reykjanes peninsula, to the the deeply indented older rock of the West Fjords, which form the northwest tip of Europe. To the south, the fertile floodplain of the Ölfusá and Þjórsa (Thórsa) rivers marks one end of the great geological rift which splits Iceland in two and spat up the Westmann Islands. The early settlers made their home here and there are important centres of history at Þingvellir (Thingvellir), Reykholt and of course, the capital, Reykjavík.

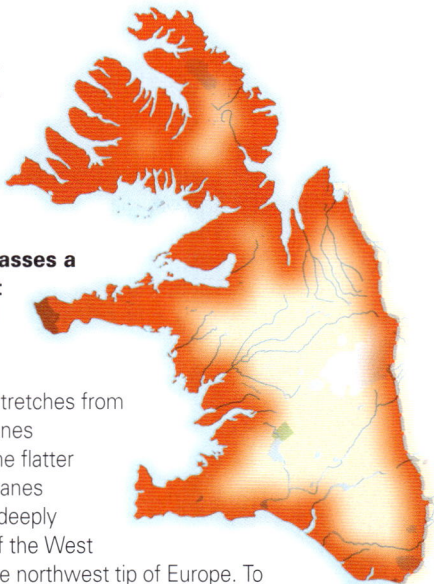

Reykjavík

Iceland's capital city is pleasingly unique. In the haphazard streets around the old harbour, the colourful old painted buildings of wood and tin give it the appearance of a frontier town, and are a reminder that Reykjavík barely appeared on the map before the end of the 18th century. It has no grand buildings like other European capitals, for Iceland was a poor country before the last century.

But the unsophisticated, homely feel is deceptive: the locals publish and read more books per head than anywhere else in the world; and they embrace new technological gadgetry with an enthusiasm that borders on the obsessive and leaves bigger, more entrenched countries of Europe lumbering in their wake. Paradoxically, they work long hours and hard (often with extra summer jobs) to maintain an admirably high standard of living; yet

they retain a broad world view and a laid-back attitude to life, a healthy resistance to authority, a sense of fun and mischief; they drink to get drunk and are sentimental about a country small enough to behave like a community.

There's plenty to enjoy here on a short break, with surprisingly good shopping, excellent restaurants and lots of good small museums and galleries to explore which are dominated by 20th-century art. The famous nightlife kicks off on a Friday and Saturday around 11pm and nobody goes home before 5am.

Temperatures are generally mild; around freezing point in winter, 11°C (52°F) in summer. In the clear, constant light of a summer's evening Reykjavík's a fascinating place. On a snowy winter's night, with candlelight glowing through every window, it's enchanting.

www.visitreykjavík.is

➕ 18J ❓ City sightseeing bus tours operate May to mid-Sep; www.re.is

ℹ️ Tourist Information, The Centre, Aðalstræti 2, 101 Reykjavík ☎ 590 1550

ÁRBÆJARSAFN (REYKJAVÍK CITY MUSEUM)

For a glimpse into lives of the past, this open-air museum site is nosy-parkers' heaven. Since 1957 interesting old houses have been migrating – lock, stock and barrel – from the centre of Reykjavík to form a unique historical collection to the east of the city. The original farmstead of Árbær, with its turf roof, has been joined by buildings of timber, stone and iron-cladding from all across Iceland. The church, which was brought here from Skagafjörður, dates from 1842 and is a picturesque spot for summer wedding parties. You can go into many of the houses to enjoy the period furnishings; often you feel that the real owner has just slipped into the next room. Traditional craft days bring the old skills to life – join in the haymaking and butter-churning and watch the blacksmith at work.

www.reykjavikmuseum.is

✚ *Reykjavík 8e* (off map) ✉ Kistuhylur 4 ☎ 411 6300
🕓 Jun–Aug daily 10–5; regular afternoon tours in winter
✋ Inexpensive 🚌 5, 6, 12, 24 ❓ Look for demonstration and craft days. Milking takes place at 4.30 every day. Guided tours in winter Mon, Wed, Fri 1–2

ÁSMUNDARSAFN (ÁSMUNDUR SVEINSSON SCULPTURE GALLERY)

The extraordinary whitewashed building with its golf-ball dome, likened to an igloo, was designed and built in the 1940s by the artist as his home and studio. It's now a museum to him, but his work is at its most impressive in the outdoor sculpture garden. Sveinsson (1893–1982) studied in Copenhagen and Paris and became one of Iceland's leading popular sculptors. He took his inspiration from the sagas, nature and the oddities of people in everyday life, and his abstract work explores a variety of styles. You'll recognize his distinctively bold and primitive forms everywhere.

www.listasafnreykjavikur.is

✚ *Reykjavík 8c* ✉ Sigtún ☎ 553 2155; ◷ May–Sep daily 10–4; Oct–Apr daily 1–4 ✋ Inexpensive, free Mon 🚌 5 from Lækjartorg and Hlemmur ❓ Part of Reykjavík Art Museum

AUSTURVÖLLUR

This peaceful leafy square, surrounded by shops and restaurants, lies at the heart of the old town on the site where Ingólfur Arnarson, the man known as the First Settler, had his hay meadows in around AD874 – the name means 'east field'. Given this historical provenance, it is entirely appropriate that the modest grey stone Alþingishús (parliament building) of 1881 should form the southern side. Some 63 MPs meet in the modern building next door from Monday to Thursday, with a Prime Minister and an elected president at their head. The statue in the centre of the square is of Jón Sigurðsson (1811–79), hero of the call for independence from Denmark in 1855; in his honour, National (Independence) Day is celebrated on 17 June, his birthday. The elegant little Dómkirkjan with its square tower is the Lutheran cathedral, built in 1796. Hótel Borg, along the east side, is Iceland's oldest and most splendid hotel.

➕ *Reykjavík 3d* ✉ Between Kirkjustræti, Vallarstræti and Pósthússtræti 🍴 Cafés and restaurants (£–£££). Try a window seat in the Café Paris for a great view of the square, or Sunday sushi at Thorvaldsen Bar

BERNHÖFTSTORFAN

A cluster of some of Reykjavík's oldest surviving buildings provides a charming centre for the Kleif Travel Market and tourist office and the Lækjarbrekka restaurant. Dating from the end of the 18th century, this is an appealing group of wooden houses with Lækjartorg square just below. To the right down broad Lækjargata is an imposing white building with a flagpole. This is Government House (Stjórnarraðið), built in 1765. Formerly a prison workhouse, it now provides offices for the Prime Minister. On the little hill beside it stands a dramatic statue by Einar Jónsson (► 84) of Ingólfur Arnarson, the First Settler. To the left, the old grammar school was the first of its kind in Iceland, and lists Nobel-prize winning author Halldór Laxness (► 11) among former pupils.

✚ *Reykjavík 3d* ✉ Kleif Travel Market and Internet café ☎ 510 5700 🍴 Lækjarbrekka (£–£££)

ELLIÐAÁRDALUR

Iceland prides itself on its policies of clean energy sources and conservation, both of which come together very successfully in this green valley lined with trees to the east of the city centre. It's a great place to escape the traffic, with a network of footpaths and cycle tracks. Running through its heart is the sparkling and unpolluted Elliðaá, site of Iceland's first hydroelectric power station and one of the best rivers for salmon in the country – rightly a source of national pride. It's the focus of the traditional opening of the fishing season on 1 May, and you can see the salmon spawning in early August. Many Icelandic horses are stabled here.

✚ *Reykjavík 8e* (off map) ✋ Free 🚌 3, 4, 6, 7, 9, 10, 11, 12, 14, 15, 110, 111, 112, 115

HALLGRÍMSKIRKJA

See pages 40–41.

HÖFN (OLD HARBOUR)

You might expect to find Reykjavík's harbour along Hafnarstræti (harbour street), but through the 20th century the boundaries were pushed seawards and the land extended artificially to provide more space, first to Tryggvagata and now Geirsgata. You can enjoy a stroll along here and watch the fishing boats offloading in the western end, perhaps admire a cruise liner or two in the eastern end, or just sit and watch the busy world go by. A replica wooden Viking ship can often be seen here, dwarfed by the grey-painted vessels of the coastguard. Don't miss the weekend fleamarket, **Kolaportið,** in

the old Tollhús building with its beautiful mosaic wall on Tryggvagata. The market is full of bric-à-brac and clothing, with an excellent little food section selling fish and local delicacies.

✚ *Reykjavík 3e* 🚌 2, 3, 4, 5, 6, 7, 110, 112, 115 ❓ Annual Festival of the Sea celebrated in the old harbour

Kolaportið

✉ Tryggragata 19 ☎ 562 5030 🕐 Sat–Sun 11–5 🍴 Café great for coffee and sandwiches (£)

KJARVALSSTAÐIR (KJARVAL COLLECTION)

The art gallery, in Miklatún Park, is primarily home to a collection of surreal landscapes by Iceland's most famous artist, Jóhannes S Kjarval (1885–1972). Kjarval began his working life as a trawlerman but his skills as a painter were quickly recognized by his colleagues, who together raised the funds necessary for his study abroad, in London and Copenhagen. Stand back a little from the paintings for the best effect.

www.listafnreykjuvikur.is

✚ *Reykjavík 5b* ✉ Flókagata ☎ 517 1290
🕐 Daily 10–5 ✋ Inexpensive, free Mon 🍴 Café
🚌 11, 12, 13 ❓ Part of Reykjavík Art Museum

LAUGARDALUR

Within walking distance of downtown Reykjavík, this is the city's main sports and recreation ground and it buzzes with families at weekends. The football stadium is here, as well as a fabulous outdoor **swimming pool** complete with waterslide, whirlpool and 'hot-pots' (geothermally heated, of course). For children, there's all the fun of the Norse and Viking-themed Family Park and Zoo (► 62), where you can stroke Icelandic horses

and encounter other friendly beasts including seals and reindeer. This is also the home of the **botanic gardens,** proof that Iceland's short growing season, unfriendly climate and volcanic soil are no obstacle to a wide range of plants and trees. Enjoy a picnic in the elegant heated pavilion. **Lauger Health and Spa Resort,** on Sundlaugavegur, is the biggest in Europe.
🚩 *Reykjavík 8c* 🚌 2–14

Swimming pool
🕐 Mon–Fri 6.50am–9.30pm, Sat–Sun 8am–10pm

Botanic gardens
🕐 Greenhouse and pavilion
Apr–Sep 10–10; Oct–Mar 10–5
✋ Free

Lauger Health and Spa Resort
☎ 553 0000; www.laugarspa.is
🕐 Mon–Fri 6am–11pm, Sat
8–10, Sun 8–8

LISTASAFN ÍSLANDS (NATIONAL GALLERY)

This tall white building with its high arched-eyebrow windows overlooks the Tjörn (➤ 88) and was originally a storage place for ice, cut from the pond and kept for use in the preservation of fish. It has been renovated in a light and modern style with lots of glass and wood-block floors to house the national collection of paintings and sculpture, which mostly date from the 20th century and include works by artists such as Nina Tryggvadóttir. It's not the biggest gallery, but the exhibitions change regularly.
www.listasafn.is
🚩 *Reykjavík 3c* ✉ Fríkirkjuvegur 7 ☎ 515 9620 🕐 Tue–Sun
11–5 🍴 Café (£) 🚌 2, 3, 4, 5, 6, 7, 110, 111, 112, 115
✋ Inexpensive, free Wed

a walk in the town centre/shore

From the statue of Leif the Lucky (➤ 11), head down Skólavörðustígur.

This is an interesting street with lots of intriguing crafts galleries and jewellers, as well as the little stone gaol.

Bear right down Klapparstígur, and turn right at the bottom onto Laugavegur.

This is Reykjavík's main shopping street, full of boutiques and, increasingly, bars.

Turn left onto Frakkastígur, with views up to the Hallgrímskirkja and down to the steel Viking ship sculpture, Sólfar, by Jón Gunnar Árnason (1931–89). At the bottom of the hill cross the busy road and turn left to follow the harbour path.

There are great views across the bay and to Mount Esja, with the harbour ahead.

Keep right past the harpoon-head sculpture and continue with the fishing harbour opening out on your right to the sculpture of two fishermen. Turn right here and continue along the harbour, then bear left into Tryggvagata, which hooks you back towards the town centre. Turn right into the square, passing the Tourist Information Centre (toilets up to your right, free).

There are lots of bars and restaurants around this popular downtown area.

Keep right and turn up Aðalstræti, passing some of the city's oldest houses on your right. Pass the old well and pump, and turn left across a paved square to enter Austurvöllur square. Pass the old parliament building on your right, and go stright on, to turn left onto Lækjargata towards the harbour. Turn right up Bankastræti, and bear diagonally right up Skólavörðustígur to return to the Hallgrímskirkja.

Distance 3km (2 miles)
Time Allow at least half a day, longer to explore properly
Start/end point Hallgrímskirkja 🚌 *Reykjavík 4c* 🚌 2, 3, 4, 5, 6, 7 from Lækjartorg, every 30 minutes in summer
Lunch Sólon (£) ✉ Bankastræti 7A ☎ 562 3232

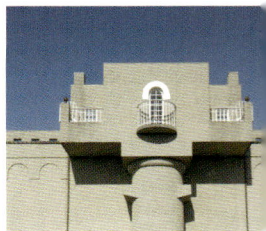

LISTASAFN EINARS JÓNSSONAR (EINAR JÓNSSON SCULPTURE MUSEUM)

High on the top of Skólavörðuholt hill, Iceland's outstanding sculptor Einar Jónsson (1874–1954) built a fortress-like house and gallery. The outside may be forbidding but inside is a collection of fantastical sculpted figures which demonstrate the extraordinary imagination of the artist. Mythical creatures of gigantic proportions emerge from the living rocks of the Icelandic landscape, or swoop up from the seas in breathtaking beauty. Look out for the terrifying troll figure, petrified in the sunrise, the teeth in his skull-like face already becoming basalt columns; and the famous *Outlaws* statue, inspiration for one of Halldór Laxness's oddest heroes, Bjartur of Summerhouses. There are more sculptures in the garden. The artist's living quarters are at the top of narrow spiral stairs. **www.**skulptur.is

✚ *Reykjavík 4c* ✉ Eiríksgata ☎ 551 3797 ⏱ Jun–Sep Tue–Sun 2–5; Sep–May Sat–Sun 2–5. Closed Dec–Jan. Sculpture garden: daily ✋ Inexpensive; sculpture garden free 🚌 7 ❓ Labels in Icelandic only; ask at the ticket desk for an invaluable sheet of translations

ÖSKJUHLÍÐ

A massive space-age edifice, designed by architect Ingimundur Sveinsson, squats on Öskjuhlíð hill, to the south of town. Its great towers hold 18 million litres of geothermally heated water – enough to service half the city. Between them is an exhibition space on different levels, with a café, and a mini-geyser which

shoots up from the basement. The jewel in this crown is definitely on the top, however – the reflective glass dome is actually one of Reykjavík's most exclusive dining palaces, Perlan, The Pearl. The restaurant rotates as you eat but don't worry about spilling your soup – one complete revolution takes two hours. Food with a view comes at a price, but you can go out on the balconies for free and see across to Mount Esja. The **Saga Museum** in one of the towers presents the history of Viking settlement in Iceland.

✚ *Reykjavík 5a* ✉ Perlan, Öskjuhlíð ☎ 562 0200 🕓 Daily 🏛 Free 🍴 Café (£); Perlan restaurant (£££) 🚌 13

Saga Museum
☎ 544 8086; www.sagamuseum.is

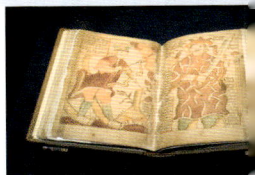

ÞJÓÐMENNING (CULTURE HOUSE)

Iceland is unique in having a written culture that goes back to its earliest days. The language, akin to Old Norse, has hardly changed over the last 1,000 years, and so the literature can be read as easily by people today as when it was written. The Sagas, complex and lively medieval tales of history, landscape, lineage and epic deeds, are still very much alive and at the heart of Icelandic culture, and this is the best place to learn more of their story. The sagas and other books were originally copied out on vellum, or calf skin. One calf skin would make just two pages, and many manuscripts ran to 200 pages and more. The manuscripts survive in books and fragments, gathered up by one man, Árni Magnússon, in the period 1702–12. They were transported to Denmark for study but unfortunately many were destroyed in the Great Fire of Copenhagen in 1728. The best were rescued, however, and in 1971 the first of these were returned to their homeland, including *Landnámabók*, *Íslandingabók*, and *Njál's Saga*. Look out for the tiny wood-bound *Margaret's Saga*.

www.thjodmenning.is

✚ *Reykjavík 4d* ✉ Hverfisgata 15 ☎ 545 1400 🕐 Daily 11–5
✋ Inexpensive 🍴 Cafe (£) ❓ Temporary exhibitions on top floor

ÞJÓÐMINJASAFN ÍSLANDS (NATIONAL MUSEUM)

This is the country's treasure house, fully refurbished in 2004. The Making of a Nation imaginatively displays Icelandic history and culture from the arrival of the first Viking settlers by boat, its scale inlaid in the wooden floor. Labelling and interactivity in English are excellent, culminating in an amusing array of 20th-century items presented on a slowly circulating airport carousel – to indicate modern Iceland's gateway to the world.

www.nationalmuseum.is

✚ *Reykjavík 2c* ✉ Suðurgata 41 ☎ 530 2200 🕐 May to mid-Sep daily 11–5; mid-Sep to Apr Tue–Sun 11–5; first Sun of month till 9pm
✋ Inexpensive 🍴 Café

TJÖRNIN

Of all Reykjavik's open spaces the area around the Tjörn, or pond, is one of the most fun. Some 40 species of birds breed here, despite its city-centre location; the sound of ducks, geese and swans waiting to be fed will lead you straight to it. A walkway runs below the main road (Fríkirkjuvegur) offering good views of the old houses opposite. The big grey building at the northern end is the controversial City Hall – inside there's a tourist information desk and an exhibition area used mainly for photography and art. Locals say the best view of the lake is from the coffee shop – because you can't see the ugly modern lines of the City Hall itself.

✚ *Reykjavík 3c* 🚌 2, 3, 4, 5, 6, 7, 110, 111, 112, 115 ✉ Tourist Information, City Hall ☎ 563 2005 🕐 Mon–Fri 8.20–4.30, Sat noon–6pm; also Sun noon–6pm May–Sep 🖐 Free 🍴 Café in City Hall (£)

VIÐEY

The citizens of Reykjavík come to this romantic island to get away from it all. Low-lying and green, it's ten minutes off shore and easily explored in a day. The island boasts a top restaurant too — you can come out just for the evening and be ferried home again at the end of your meal.

There was once a monastery here and the island is full of history. Around 1755 entrepreneur and Royal Superintendent Skúli Magnússon had a stone house built as a sign of wealth and confidence (the oldest original building in Iceland, now restored to hold the restaurant); his attempts to turn the fortunes of Reykjavík failed and he died bankrupt in 1794 – there's a memorial to him by the church. A small community made the island their home in the last century, centring their hopes on a fishery, but it too failed and now the village is deserted.

✚ 18J ✉ Kollafjörður

🍴 Viðeyjarstofa ☎ 562 1934: afternoon coffee and cake, restaurant (booking essential) 🚢 Ferry from Sundahöfn or Midbakki ☎ 533 5055 for information and booking

❓ Can be combined on a half-day trip with a visit to the puffin island of Lundey

YLSTRÖDIN NAUTHÓLSVÍK

Golden sands and coastal swimming are not what you expect to find in Iceland. But here, in the shadow of Reykjavík airport, a facility offering just that opened in 2000. The sand comes from Skaftafell and the water is geothermally heated to 19–20°C (66–68°F) in the lagoon.

✚ *Reykjavík 4a* (off map) ✉ South of Öskjuhlíð ☎ 511 6630 🕐 May–Sep 10–10 💰 Free, but small charge for use of changing rooms

What to See in the West

ARNARSTAPI

The delightful cove of Arnarstapi is perfectly set on the end of the great Snæfellsnes peninsula, its steep cliffs and stacks home to a myriad of screaming sea birds, its wooden holiday cottages all turned to face the view and the sunshine. As you turn down towards the sheltered harbour, you can't miss the gigantic boulderous, be-hatted figure on the clifftop to your right. He's Bárður Snæfellsás, a spirit who lives in the great mountain of Snæfellsjökull which shelters the village to the north. The cliffs are riddled with blow-holes and echoing caves and, to the west, there's a natural stone arch. The coastline is a nature reserve, and from the car park above the harbour you can take the footpath to neighbouring Hellnar. A small community of New Age enthusiasts live here, attracted by the supposed magic properties of the mountain.

✚ 2A ✉ On southwest end of Snæfellsnes peninsula, Route 574 🍴 Snjófell restaurant at Arnarstapi (£–££); café and hotel at Hellnar (££–£££) 🚤 Boat trips and whale-watching from Ólafsvík, contact Sæferðir-Eyjaferðir ☎ 438 1450 ❓ For cycle hire, snowmobiling and camping contact Snjófell, Arnarstapi ☎ 435 6783; www.snjofell.is

BLÁA LÓNIÐ (BLUE LAGOON)
See pages 34–35.

BORGARNES

Travelling northwards on Route 1 you turn a corner to see the pretty town of Borgarnes stretched out along its narrow peninsula on the opposite shore of Borgarfjörður. In its beautiful but exposed location, with the plains of Myrar behind and the mountains to the west and south, it catches all the available light and sunshine. This is Iceland's biggest non-fishing town. A little white church with a dark-hatted steeple dominates the skyline, giving it an unexpectedly Alpine air. There are strong connections in this area with *Egil's Saga*, and Egil's father Skallagrímur was buried in the town's triangle of green park, with his horse and other accoutrements as befitted a great chief. The relief depicts Egil himself, carrying the body of his son Böðvar, who drowned near by. The farm and church at Borg á Mýrum, just north of Borgarnes, mark the spot where the body of Egil's grandfather, Kveldúlfur, was washed ashore in its coffin, setting a good omen for his settler family.

✚ 18K ✉ On Route 1, 74km (46 miles) north of Reykjavík 🍴 Hótel Borgarnes (££) 🚌 All Reykjavík buses pass through on their way to the West fjords or Akureyri 🛈 Tourist Information Centre at Hyrnan service centre ☎ 437 1224; www.west.is

BÚDARDALUR

This unassuming farming community at the head of
Hvammsfjörður marks the gateway to Laxárdalur –
the salmon river valley and setting for Iceland's
most romantic Laxdæla Saga. The tale is set around
the tragic love of two foster brothers, Kjartan and
Bolli, for the lovely Guðrun Ósvífursdóttir. A replica
Viking longhouse has been built at **Eiríksstaðir,** the
birth place of adventurer Leifur Eiríksson, and in
summer, costumed staff bring his story to life.

✚ 5B ✉ On Route 60, 154km (95 miles) north of Reykjavík

Eiríksstaðir

☎ 434 1118; www.leif.is ◷ Jun–Sep daily 9–6
✋ Inexpensive

FLATEY

See pages 36–37.

GULLFOSS AND GEYSIR

See pages 38–39.

HAFNARFJÖRÐUR

Overshadowed by neighbouring
Reykjavík, Hafnarfjörður has
always boasted a better natural
harbour and has been a busy
fishing port for over 60 years. It
hosts the Hafnarfjörður Museum,
but is perhaps best known locally
as the town which takes elves
seriously. So seriously, in fact, that roads have been diverted to
avoid upsetting the little people. Thanks to the work of a local seer,
there's now a 'Hidden World' map available at the tourist
information centre showing pixie hot-spots around the town.

Hafnarfjörður is also the centre for modern Viking activities, offering an imaginative Viking-themed restaurant, Fjörukráin, in a magnificent old wooden house down by the harbour. This is the focus for the riotous activities of the international Viking Festivals, and some pretty lively behaviour on Friday and Saturday nights too.
www.hafnarfjordur.is

🚌 18J 🍴 Full range of cafés and restaurants (£–£££) 🚢 Short and long sea trips available, including whale-watching and sea-angling ❓ International Viking Festival about every two years, last held 2006 ☎ 565 1213; www.vikingvillage.is

ℹ️ Strandgata 6 ☎ 585 5500 ⏰ Daily 8–5; also Jul–Aug Sat–Sun 10–5

93

HAFNIR

The Reykjanes peninsula marks the southwestern end of the great geological fault which runs diagonally across the country. On its furthest tip is the scattered former fishing village of Hafnir. You can discover more about Iceland's piscatorial heritage at the fascinating **aquarium,** well stocked with local sea and freshwater fish. Look out for the anchor of the ghost ship *Jamestown*; abandoned off the coast of America in 1867, it drifted ashore here three years later, complete with its cargo of timber. To the south, the rocks swarm with migrant and nesting birds, including gannets from the offshore island of Eldey.

www.reykjanes.is

🕂 17J 🖼 Whale-spotting trips from Keflavík ☎ 421 7777

🏦 Hafnagata 57 ☎ 421 6777

Sæfiskasafnið (Aquarium)

☎ 421 6958 🕐 Jun–Aug daily 2–5.30; Sep–May daily 2–4

✋ Inexpensive

HEKLA

The country's most infamous – and still very active – volcano last erupted in March 2000, and Icelanders are holding their breath waiting for the big one. It is known to erupt about every ten years, with the last major eruption in 1991, but scientists suspect that recent rumblings may herald a new period of activity. The volcano forms a ridged mountain 1,491m (4,890ft) high on the great geological rift which divides Iceland, looming over the lowlands of the southwest with its top usually hidden modestly away in cloud. In the Middle Ages it was notorious throughout Europe as the gateway to hell. Visit the **Hekla Centre** and watch the audiovisual explanations to learn more.

🕂 21J

Hekla Centre

✉ Brúarlandur, off Route 26 ☎ 487 6591 🕐 All year (ring for opening times) ✋ Inexpensive

HELLISSANDUR

Set on the northwestern tip of the Snæfellsnes peninsula, on the edge of the black lava field that flows down from Snæfellsjökull, this town has spectacular views to the cliffs of the West Fjords. At the **museum** you can explore an old fisherman's hut and boat, and there are lots of paths and tracks to follow amid the lava. Hellissandur's biggest claim to fame is the towering radio mast, 412m (1,351ft) high, which was the tallest structure in Europe when it was built in 1959. In such a windy place, the mast would have snapped off had it been dug into the ground, so instead it is balanced on a point and held up by wires. Spare a thought for the two people (one a woman) who keep its paintwork fresh.

➕ 2B ✉ On Route 574, 245km (152 miles) northwest of Reykjavík

Sjómannagarðurinn við Útnesveg (Museum)

✉ Útnesvegur ☎ 436 6961 🕐 Jun–Aug daily 9–6 ✋ Inexpensive

HORNSTRANDIR

Hornstrandir has always been remote and isolated; in the days when people lived on its fjords the only way in or out was by sea, and it's the same today. Its high barren uplands, lush lowlands and rugged cliffs are protected now as a nature reserve, and the banning of sheep as well as vehicles has meant a return of the land to meadow and wildflowers. To reach this hiker's paradise, catch the boat from Ísafjörður, making sure you have everything you need with you for several days – there's no accommodation other than emergency huts and the odd summer house, and you must be prepared for every sort of weather. You'll be rewarded by peace and, with luck, an abundance of wildlife.

www.vestfirdir.is

➕ 5F ✉ Northern tip of West Fjords, access on foot or by boat only

🛥 Scenic boat trips and tours from Ísafjörður

ℹ️ Aðalstræti 7, Ísafjörður ☎ 456 5121

HÚSAFELL

This beautiful spot near the head of a long valley is covered in low birch trees and littered with gaily painted summer houses, testament to its warm temperatures and handy supply of natural hot water. A popular centre for camping, it is set about with attractive wilderness and icecaps, notably Eiríksjökull, Langjökull and Ok. You can take the high road over to Kaldidalur or hike from the valley head to explore the lava caves – the longest, Kalmanshellir, is 4km (2.5 miles).

✚ 19L ✉ On Route 518, east of Reykholt ☎ 435 1550 (accommodation) 🍴 Snack bar (£–££) 🚌 Daily bus in summer from Reykjavík via Þingvellir and Kaldidalur ❓ Guided walks to the caves ☎ 435 1558

Rekjavík to Húsafell

Explore small towns, a beautiful long valley and a spectacular fjord.

Take Route 1 north from Reykjavík, via Mosfellsbær. At Hvalfjörður follow signs for the tunnel (toll payable). At the other side, turn left onto Route 51 to Akranes. Turn off before Akranes on the 503 for the Araknes Museum (▶ 100). Head north on Route 51. Turn left and left again, and follow Route 1 to Borgarnes (▶ 91).

To the left, the fertile plains are dotted with farms; to your right are sweeping fells of black scree, giving way to bushy vegetation.

Cross the scenic causeway to Borgarnes and stay on Route 1 towards Akureyri.

This beautiful wide valley is a popular holiday spot, with marked walking trails. Great viewpoint at Svignaskarð.

Turn right at the octagonal service station, Baulan, on Route 50 to Reykholt. Stay on this road, signed to Reykholt, then bear left towards Reykholt on the 518 after 5km (3 miles).

Explore the church, museum centre and Snorri's pool (► 104). The Fosshótel Reykholt is just behind.

Continue on Route 518 to Húsafell (► 97), passing the lovely Hraunfossar waterfalls on your left. Stay on the 518 around the head of the valley. At Brúará bridge, stay on the 523 to pass a café at Bjarnastaðir; at the junction with the 522 turn left, and right onto Route 50 to Borgarnes. Turn left onto Route 1 and retrace route south to the junction with Route 47. Turn left here for Hvalfjörður (► 100) and take the old road around this fabulous fjord. Rejoin Route 1 and return to Reykjavík.

Distance 300km (186 miles)
Time Allow a full day, or take it slowly over two days
Start/end point A circular route from Reykjavík ✚ 18J
Lunch Fosshótel Reykholt (££)

HVALFJÖRÐUR

It is said that you may see up to 17 species of whale in this deep fjord during late summer. The whales were particularly welcomed in days gone by – you can see something of the history of local whaling (which stopped in 1989 and then resumed in 2003) and 'Cod Wars' at the excellent **Araknes Museum.** This narrow finger of water is sheltered by Mount Esja to the south and Skarðsheiði to the north and, now that it has been bypassed by the tunnel at Saurbær, it has returned to something like tranquillity, with only the ferro-silicon smelter on the northern shore to mar its beauty. Irish monks were the first settlers here, commemorated by a stone in the cemetery at Akranes. It's difficult to imagine this peaceful place bristling with naval hardware, but during World War II the Allies had a massive base here and it was a key location for the North Atlantic convoys.

✛ 18K ✉ 43km (27 miles) north of Reykjavík

Akranes Museum

✉ Garður, by Akranes ☎ 431 5566; www.museum.is 🕐 May–Sep daily 10–6; Sep–Apr daily 1–6 🖐 Moderate 🍴 Café in the Museum Hall

HVERAGERÐI

You'll notice that there are no tower blocks in this town – it's built on the edge of an active geothermal area and small earthquakes are commonplace. Steam from the naturally hot water (reaching 200°C/392°F underground) is used to heat greenhouses – pause at Eden on Austurmörk for souvenirs and a taste of tropical plantlife. There's good walking in the hills, and a geothermal area in the town centre with boiling mud pots and sulphurous fumaroles. You could even treat yourself to a mud bath at the health spa. One spring is named Ruslahver, or 'garbage hot spring', after the rubbish that had been tipped down it when it was a dry hole resurfaced during an earthquake.

✚ 19J ✉ On Route 1, 38km (24 miles) southeast of Reykjavík ♭ Café with pastries to die for at Hverabakarí (bakery), Breiðamörk 10

ℹ South Iceland Information Centre, Sunnumörk ☎ 483 4601; www.southiceland.is

HVOLSVÖLLUR

In the flat, fertile land north of the Thverá River lies the village of Hvolsvöllur, all too easily bypassed by the hurrying tourist anxious for the next great sight. Instead, pause awhile, for you are entering the magical country of one of the greatest of epics, *Njál's Saga*,

and the **Saga Centre** here will help you to make sense of it all. As well as exhibitions explaining the characters, the story and its locations, the centre sets this best-loved Saga in the context of the Viking age. Story telling was once a fundamental part of Icelandic life and is revived here in a specially re-created medieval hall.

✚ 20H ✉ 106km (66 miles) southeast of Reykjavík

Sögusetrið (Saga Centre)

✉ Hliðarveg ☎ 487 8781; www.njala.is 🕐 Jun–Aug daily 9–5 ♭ Hlíðarendi restaurant (£–££) ✋ Inexpensive ❓ Musical presentation in various languages Jul–Aug 7pm; booking essential

ÍSAFJÖRÐUR

Dramatically set on its own inlet of the wide Ísafjarðarjúp fjord and sheltered by mountains, Ísafjörður is the capital of the remote West Fjords region. It is the jumping-off point for a wide range of activities including mini-cruises, whale-watching, hiking and sea-angling in summer, and skiing in winter, and is also the gateway to Hornstrandir (➤ 96). The town was one of Iceland's key trading ports from 1569 to the early 19th century, and a complex of four old wooden houses, now a maritime museum, on the seafront bears testament to this. Cod, shark and herring were all sought with Þilskip (thilskip) – small boats with decks – instead of the more common open rowing boats.

www.isafjordur.is

✚ 3E ✉ 457km (283 miles) north of Reykjavík

ℹ Aðalstræti 7

☎ 456 5121

🕐 Mon–Fri 8–6, and summer weekends 10–3

KRÝSUVÍK

Iceland has around 200 volcanoes and 250 natural hot springs, and has produced about one third of the total world lava flow in the last 400 years. If you've only got a short time to visit Iceland, then this is the most interesting geothermal site near Reykjavík where you can stroll among smelly steam holes and horribly bubbling mud pools – it's no surprise to learn that sulphur was once mined here. The gloriously multi-coloured volcanic scoria beneath your feet can be hot and uncertain, so be careful where you tread and stick to the boardwalks. The whole area is part of the Reykjanesfólkvangur national reserve.

✚ 18H ✉ South of Reykjavík on Route 42

LÁTRABJARG

Nowhere in Iceland are the sea birds so tightly packed along the cliffs as here, on the westernmost point of Europe. This older rock, in a sheer, undulating line of cliffs that stretch some 11km (7 miles) and rise to 511m (1,676ft) high, has been worn and ground on its exposed seaward surface to form natural ledges, which are like high-rise penthouses to a vast density of kittiwakes and fulmars, guillemots, puffins and one-third of the world's total population of razorbills. From a distance it is like watching a swarming beehive as the birds fly up and down and out to sea, and close up the noise of their calling is incredible. In days gone by, hardy locals would lower themselves over the edge on a rope to collect the eggs in a test of bravery, skill and basic survival.

✚ 1D ✉ Western tip of the West Fjords

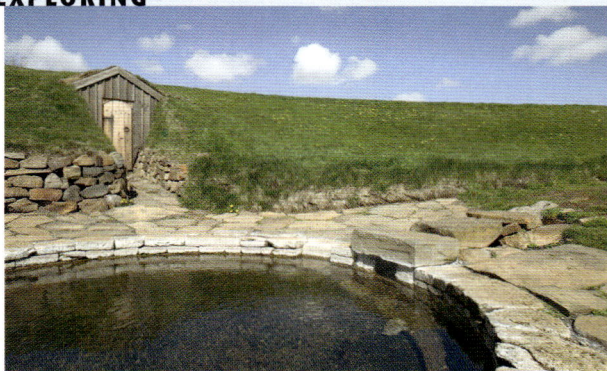

REYKHOLT

The greatest of Icelandic writers Snorri Sturluson (➤ 11) lived in this beautiful rolling valley from 1206–41, composing his mighty history of Norwegian kings, *Heimskringla*. He had his own thermal bathing pool, Snorralaug, once linked straight to his farm by a tunnel, which you can see steaming beyond the church. The **Modern Centre for Medieval Research** is dedicated to him – with its tall-hatted spire, it's a distinctive landmark. A statue of Snorri stands outside the former grammar school, now home to the National Library.

✚ 19L ✉ Turn left off Route 527, in the Hvíta valley, 43km (27 miles) east of Borgarnes

Snorrastofa-Heimskringla (Modern Centre for Medieval Research)
✉ 320 Reykholt ☎ 435 1490; www.reykholt.is ✪ May–Sep daily 10–6; Oct–Apr Mon–Fri 10–5 ✖ Fosshótel Reykholt behind old farmstead
❓ Car parks below centre and futher along main road; centre is focus of an annual music festival in July

SKÁLHOLT

The stark white **church** at Skálholt stands out of the green landscape like a beacon. It is only 50 years old but there have been similar buildings on this important site for centuries since one of the country's first two bishoprics was founded here in 1056. In 1550 the community was taught a sharp lesson when rebel Catholic bishop Jón Arason was summarily beheaded for opposing

the introduction of Lutheranism from Denmark. Skálholt remained a (now Lutheran) bishopric until a general migration to Reykjavík at the end of the 18th century. In the church you can admire the massive stone sarcophagus of another early bishop, Páll Jónsson, and the striking modern mosaic of Christ by artist Nina Tryggvadóttir. Archaeological excavations around the church are revealing the scale of the original farming settlement.

🔶 20J ✉ Northeast of Selfoss on Route 31, just north of Laugarás
Church
✉ Biskupstungur, 801 Selfoss ☎ 486 8870 🕑 Daily
❓ Free concerts at weekends in Jul and Aug

SNÆFELLSJÖKULL

On a clear day you can see the iced pixie-hat peak of this mountain, apparently floating weightless above the sea, all the way from Reykjavík. It's not the biggest glacier in the country but one of the most appealing and accessible. Perched on the end of the long ridge of Snæfellsnes, the views from the top are fantastic. Jules Verne picked it as the gateway to the underworld in *Journey to the Centre of the Earth* (he obviously hadn't been through the 6.4km/ 4-mile Hvalfjördur tunnel), and even today it revels in a dubious mystical reputation which acts as a magnet for New Agers and free spirits. You can get to the top fairly easily from Arnarstapi or Ólafsvík by snowmobile or skidoo – make sure you stick to your guide's tracks in summer, when crevasses can be dangerous. It's a popular spot for family picnics and tobogganing.
www.ust.is

🔶 2A ✉ Western tip of Snæfellsnes, 195km (121 miles) northwest of Reykjavík ❓ Glacier trips from Arnarstapi (➤ 90) and Ólafsvík
ℹ Snæfellsjökull National Park Visitor Centre, Hellnar ☎ 436 6860

STYKKISHÓLMUR

This windblown town on the north shore of Snæfellsnes is an odd mixture of good, bad and plain ugly. Approaching by road, you see the sweeping white pylon 'H' of the church off to your right, a lively and daring piece of modern architecture. There are some splendid old wooden houses down by the harbour, including the black-painted Norwegian House of 1832, now a museum and gallery but built as the home of Iceland's first meteorologist, Árni Thorlacius. The old centre is dominated by the looming ochre walls of a Franciscan convent, however, which seems out of place amid the gaily painted houses. Paganism has always had a place here and to prove it there's a magical hill, Helgafell, where – if you follow the rules – you may be granted three wishes. Look out for scallop shells in the bay; the other local speciality is traditionally cured shark *(hákarl)* – follow your nose westwards to Bjarnarhöfn.

www.stykkisolmur.is

✚ 3B ✉ At the end of Route 58 🍴 Several restaurants and snack bars 🚢 Ferry sailings and tours ☎ 438 1450 ❓ Baldur, the car and passenger ferry across Breiðafjörður bay to Flatey and the West Fjords, leaves here on its daily circuit. Also whale-watching tours, bird-watching tours and scallop fishing

🛈 Borgarbraut ☎ 438 1150

ÞINGVELLIR (THINGVELLIR)
See pages 50–51.

ÞÓRSMÖRK (THORSMORK)
One of the world's great treks, that from the extraordinary lunarscape of Landmannalaugar (➤ 110), leads over the mountains to this remote and beautiful nature reserve set about with birch woods, entwined rivers and superb glacier-topped scenery. It's a wilderness with its own warmer micro-climate, best explored on foot. Don't expect to drive there unless you're with an experienced group – the road into the valley crosses the powerful and dangerous Krossá River, and this is best left to the experts with their specially high-set coaches.

➕ 21H ✉ Access up F249, off Route 1 south of Hvolsvöllur

VESTMANNAEYJAR (WESTMANN ISLANDS)
See pages 52–53.

HOTELS

REYKJAVÍK

Baldursbrá (£–££)

Friendly guest house offering comfortable and spacious bed and breakfast accommodation in a quiet quarter within a few minutes' walk of the town centre. Proprietors Joachim and Ariane Fischer are funds of local knowledge. Free transfer available to and from airport bus.

✉ Laufásvegur 41 ☎ 552 6646 🕐 All year

Hóll Cottage (£££)

This lovely historic cottage on a side street in the centre of town offers you a quiet space to call your own within easy walking distance of all the main attractions. Beautifully restored and thoughtfully equipped, sleeps 4–6, self-catering.

✉ Grjótagata 12 ☎ 864 4481; www.simnet.is/holl 🕐 All year

Hótel Borg (£££)

Iceland's oldest and smartest hotel, restored to 1930s art deco splendour, and complete with ballroom. Every bedroom is decorated with a different theme. A new top floor was added in 2006.

✉ Pósthússtræti 11 ☎ 551 1440; www.hotelborg.is 🕐 All year

Hótel Holt (£££)

A stylish and luxurious modern hotel set discreetly amid the international embassies in a gracious part of the town centre. Boasts a fine restaurant, as well as modern art on every wall.

✉ Bergstaðastræti 37 ☎ 552 5700; www.holt.is 🕐 All year

BORGARNES

Bjarg (£–££)

Comfortable bed and breakfast accommodation in a splendid old gabled farmhouse outside the town; good walking in the area.

✉ By Borgarnes ☎ 437 1925 🕐 All year

LÁTRABJARG
Breiðavík (£–££)
Simple bed and breakfast accommodation in a renovated former schoolhouse. Convenient for exploring the bird cliffs, and offers fishing permits for the local lakes.

✉ Látrabjarg ☎ 456 1575; www.breidavik.net ◷ May–Sep

SNÆFELLSNES
Hotel Hellnar (££–£££)
This pleasant, timber-clad hotel has been certified for its policy of sustainable eco-tourism since 2002, and offers glacier tours and horse riding as well as fabulous views over the coastline. Next door to the National Park Visitor Centre.

✉ Brekkubær, Hellnar ☎ 435 6820; www.hellnar.is ◷ May–Sep, other times by arrangement

Guesthouse Langaholt (£–££)
You're guaranteed a friendly welcome at this family hotel, in a fantastic setting on a long sandy beach with its own 9-hole golf course and views to the Snæfell glacier. Variety of rooms and facilities available, from sleeping-bag up to a high standard of comfort with your own bathroom.

✉ Garðar ☎ 435 6789; www.langaholt.is ◷ Mar–Nov

RESTAURANTS

REYKJAVÍK
A Naestu Grosum (£)
Excellent downtown vegetarian restaurant, with buffet-style section, home-made bread and cakes and organic wines.

✉ Laugavegur 20b ☎ 552 8410 ◷ Mon–Sat lunch and dinner, Sun dinner only

Café Paris (£)
The green building on the corner of Austervöllur square – get yourself a window table and watch the world go by. Can be very busy. Pancakes with ice-cream are especially good.

✉ Austervöllur ☎ 551 1020 ◷ Lunch and dinner

Deli (£)

For food on the run, don't miss this little snack bar at the bottom of Skolavörðustígur. Look through to the kitchen to see your food being freshly prepared with top quality ingredients – pasta salads, panini with sundried tomatoes and mozzarella, focaccia, pizza and tasty sandwiches. Also at the University, beside the National Museum.

✉ Bankastræti 14 ☎ 551 6000; www.deli.is ◷ 10–7

Einar Ben (££–£££)

Set in the upper part of an elegant old red townhouse, above a woollen goods shop, this stylish restaurant and bar is close to the main tourist information centre. Try langoustine tails with salt cod cannelloni, or flounder fillets in a parsley crust, followed by white chocolate cheesecake with wild strawberry ice-cream.

✉ Veltusund 1 ☎ 511 5090; www.einarben.is ◷ Dinner

EldSmidjan (£)

Wonderful smells waft from the wood-fired oven as you enter this corner-set pizza house, just down from the Hallgrímskirkja. It's good, simple food at its best. Downstairs is a busy takeaway and upstairs it's cosy, with room for just a few to sit. The menus come in all the varieties you'd expect, but with some interesting variations. Try a fiery Hekla; and an *ostagerðarmannsins* (old cheesemaker) comes with mozarella, cream cheese, parmesan and blue cheese.

✉ Bragagötu 38A ☎ 562 3838 ◷ Lunch and dinner

Fylgifiskar (£–££)

Enjoy soup and a choice of three hot dishes at this remarkable seafish emporium, overlooking Laugardalur. Owner Guðbörg Glóð Logadottír has studied all aspects of fish preparation, and serves over 30 different kinds, all fresh and flavoursome, delicately spiced. You can also buy it ready prepared to cook yourself. Sesam Bleikja – Arctic char with sesame, corriander and chilli – is a speciality. Branch at Skólavörðustígur.

✉ Suðurlandsbraut 10 ☎ 533 1300 ◷ Lunch Mon–Fri, and Sat in winter

Kína-Húsið (£–£££)

If you fancy a change, try this top Chinese restaurant in the town centre. You can't miss it – it's painted bright red for luck. Sample lobster in a curry sauce, fish with bamboo shoots and mushrooms, or perhaps sweet and sour duck. Inexpensive lunchtime menus.

✉ Lækjargata 8 ☎ 551 1014 🕐 Lunch and dinner, closed Sat and Sun lunch

Lækjarbrekka (££–£££)

The old wooden house is one of Reykjavík's most popular restaurants, famous for its traditional dishes including mountain lamb and a summer lobster feast. The atmosphere is cosy behind the lace curtains, and the food delicious.

✉ Bankastræti 2 ☎ 551 4430 🕐 Lunch and dinner, and afternoon café

Perlan (£££)

Gives a whole new meaning to the term 'top restaurant', built in a revolving glass dome on the city's hot water tanks. Dining is formal but excellent – locals come here for an expensive treat.

✉ Öskjuhlíð ☎ 562 0200; www.perlan.is 🕐 Dinner daily

Restaurant Hornið (£–££)

An old golden-painted restaurant and bar high on a corner near the post office, serving a wide range of fresh seafood, pizza and pasta. The food is terrific and affordable.

✉ Hafnarstræti 15 ☎ 551 3340 🕐 Lunch and dinner

Sjávarkjallarinn (££–£££)

One of Reykjavík's newest and trendiest restaurants, in the historic setting of a stone-built cellar beneath the main tourist office. Fish dishes are prepared with oriental overtones, but meat-eaters and vegetarians are also well catered for.

✉ Adalstræti 2 ☎ 511 1212 🕐 Mon–Sat lunch and dinner, Sun dinner only

Sólon (£)

Wooden chairs, candles and art on the walls give this corner restaurant a cosmopolitan air, and it's perfectly set for a lunchtime break when you've been shopping 'til you're dropping on

Laugavegur. Sample the bread and tapenade, or perhaps the seafood soup, and leave room for the cake of the day. Good range of vegetarian choices, too.

✉ Bankastræti 7A ☎ 562 3232 🕐 Lunch and dinner

Svarta kaffið (£–££)

Upstairs bar and coffee house on Laugavegur with an unusual but very tasty lunchtime speciality – *súpa í brauði* – which is home-made soup served in a crusty bread roll. Light meals.

✉ Laugavegur 54 ☎ 551 2999 🕐 Lunch and dinner

Þrír (Thrír) Frakkar (££–£££)

A curious restaurant with a popular reputation for fish, and an owner with a distinctive sense of humour – the name can mean three Frenchmen or three overcoats, and he chose the latter. Décor has an off-beat kitsch feel – note the dried fish clock on the wall. You can taste a traditional Icelandic dish of combined fish and potato (*plokkfiskur*), served with black bread. Other fish dishes tend to be served with strong, creamy sauces. Soup of the day is included in the price. Whale meat is a speciality.

✉ Baldursgata 14 ☎ 552 3939 🕐 Lunch Mon–Fri, dinner daily

Tjarnarbakkinn (££–£££)

This romantic restaurant is found upstairs in the old theatre, the coffee-coloured tin-clad building at the end of Tjörnin by the Town Hall. The fare is traditional and the setting is charming.

✉ Vonarstræti 3 ☎ 562 9700; www.idno.is 🕐 Lunch and dinner

Við Tjörnina (£££)

The best restaurant in town for fish, you'll find it hidden down between the Tjörn and the Lutheran cathedral on the first floor of an unprepossessing place. The décor includes old lace, pretty china and home-made menus. Marinaded cod-cheeks are the house speciality and taste infinitely better than they sound. Highly recommended.

✉ Templarasund 3 ☎ 551 8666 🕐 Lunch and dinner Mon–Fri, dinner only Sat–Sun

HAFNARFJÖRÐUR

Fjörukráin (£–££)

Magnificent Viking-themed restaurant and bar by the harbour.
Bold, imaginative décor and an eccentric atmosphere.

✉ Strandgata 55 ☎ 565 1213/565 1890; www.fjorkrain.is ⊕ Lunch and dinner

ENTERTAINMENT

CINEMA

Reykjavík has several cinemas showing films in their original
language with Icelandic sub-titles.

✉ Sambia, Álfabakki 8 ☎ 587 8900; ✉ Sambia, Kringlan ☎ 588 0800
✉ Laugarásbíó, Laugarás ☎ 553 2075

LIVE ARTS

National Theatre

Quality drama. Shakespeare performed in Icelandic.

✉ Hverfisgata, Reykjavík ☎ 551 1200

Reykjavík City Theatre

Lively dance, theatre and musicals, as well as touring productions.

✉ Listabraut 3, Reykjavík ☎ 568 8000

Iceland Opera

The national opera company boasts the northernmost opera house
in the world. Limited performances in summer.

✉ Ingólfstræti, Reykjavík ☎ 511 6400/4200; www.opera.is

Iceland Symphony Orchestra

Offers world-class international programmes throughout the year.
Its new permanent home will be in the East Harbour from 2009.

✉ Háskólabíó, Reykjavík ☎ 545 2500; www.sinfonia.is

Salurinn, Kópavogur

Iceland's first purpose-built concert hall hosts a wide range of
music from chamber music to jazz.

✉ Hamraborg. Reykjavík ☎ 570 0400; www.salurinn.is

The North and Northeast

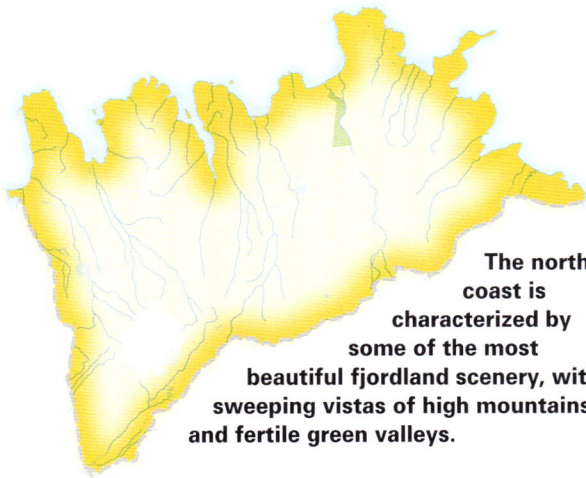

The north coast is characterized by some of the most beautiful fjordland scenery, with sweeping vistas of high mountains and fertile green valleys.

The area offers some of the country's best salmon fishing, whale-spotting and bird life, as well as the most spectacular geothermal area around Mývatn and more than its fair share of magnificent waterfalls.

The eastern part is bleaker, with rolling brown moorland, and marshland on the northern tip. In summer there is good access to the vast empty spaces of the interior, lit up by the occasional welcome oasis of green.

Akureyri

Despite its location so close to the Arctic Circle, Iceland's northern capital has the reputation of a banana belt. It may get more snow and cold weather in winter than Reykjavík, but this is more than compensated for by greater warmth and sunshine in summer. Locals make the most of this by growing trees and flowers everywhere – in tubs, window boxes and gardens – and it's known as a floral town. Artists also flourish here.

Agriculturally, this is one of the richest areas in Iceland and you'll see lots of red-roofed farms dotted along the shores of Eyjafjörður. Farmers first settled here in Viking times, when it became known as a trading area. However, the town itself only developed in the late 18th century, in two distinct halves – the old Danish town around Aðalstræti and the Icelandic town around the modern harbour. They met in the middle with the theatre in 1902, where you can still see the old harbour walls. Akureyri now boasts a population of 16,000 and its own university.

You can easily walk around the pleasant old centre in a day. There are good shops and eating places, an interesting church, a lovely botanic garden and numerous little museums to explore. Einar Jónsson's famous *Outlaws* staute stands on Eyarlandsvegur near the park (► 85). A stroll past the old houses along Aðalstræti is a must. The town claims the world's most northerly 18-hole golf course, Jaðarsvöllur, and all are welcome at the Arctic Open tournament, held through the hours of midnight sun in June.

www.eyjafjordur.is

✚ 10D ✉ 389km (241 miles) northeast of Reykjavík on Route 1 🍴 Range of eating places (£–£££) 🚌 Daily coach service from Reykjavík ☎ 462 4442; scheduled air services from Reykjavík with Air Iceland ☎ 460 7000 ⛴ Regular ferry service to Hrísey and Grímsey ☎ 462 7733 ❓ Artic Open: www.arcticopen.is ℹ Bus terminal, Hafnarstræti 82 ☎ 462 7733; 🕐 Sep–May Mon–Fri 8–5; Jun–Aug Mon–Fri 7.30–7, Sat–Sun 8–7

AKUREYRARKIRKJA

In summer a steady stream of visitors makes its way up the long flight of steps from the corner of Hafnarstræti and Kaupvangsstræti to the white-painted church at the top. With its stumpy twin towers and square front it's not Iceland's most beautiful church but it's interesting nevertheless as a forerunner of Reykjavík's Hallgrímskirkja (➤ 40–41); also designed by Guðjón Samúelsson, it was built in 1940. Inside, the stained glass shows important scenes from Icelandic history. The distinguished central window in the chancel is a survivor of the old Coventry Cathedral in England. Removed for safekeeping during World War II, it was eventually sold to an Icelander who presented it to the new church.

www.akirkja.is

☎ 462 7700 🕒 Jun–Aug 10–12 and 2–4 👋 Free ❓ Service 11am, Sunday

KJARNASKÓGAR

Carry on south of town towards the airport for a few kilometers and you'll reach this beautiful area of woodland, mainly birch and conifer, set on a sunny hillside. It's a favourite with local people at weekends – there are lots of walking trails and good places for picnics and barbecues.

✉ Just south of town on Route 821 🕒 Open access 👋 Free

MINJASAFN AKUREYRAR (FOLK MUSEUM)

The town's beautifully presented museum occupies a modern building screened by trees on Aðalstræti. Displays, including a rare ship-burial on the the ground floor, bring the history of Iceland to life. The little church below it is part of the museum, moved to this location from Svalbarðseyri on the opposite shore.

✚ 25D3 ✉ Aðalstræti 58 ☎ 462 4162; www.akmus.is 🕓 Jun–Sep daily 11–5; Sep–May Sat 2–4 ✋ Inexpensive ❓ Summer concerts held in the church

NONNAHÚS

You can pick out 'Nonni's House' on Aðalstræti from the life-size statue in the garden of the pink house in front, of a friendly looking fellow in hat and cloak. Nonni was the nickname of Jesuit priest Jón Sveinsson (1857–1944), a widely travelled man who incorporated his own adventures into stories for children which in turn became famous across Europe.

www.nonni.is

✉ Aðalstræti 54a ☎ 462 3555 🕓 Jun–Aug daily 10–5 ✋ Inexpensive

What to See in the North and Northeast

ASKJA

If you want to get into the island's remote desert interior, then this is one of the places to head for. You can do it on a day's round trip from Reykjalíð but be warned – the track is demanding and 4WD essential. Route F88 passes through a desolate landscape of gritty black lava and unwholesome powdery yellow pumice, but it's worth the trip to see this vast caldera in the Dyngjufjöll mountains. It was formed as recently as 1875 when the nearby volcano of Víti erupted, smothering much of eastern Iceland in ash. In the southeast corner of this massive natural depression is a smaller caldera, holding the windswept expanse of Öskjuvatn, at 217m (712ft) believed to be the deepest lake in the country.

Heading south on Route F88 towards Askja, you'll see a curiously symmetrical, black, flat-topped mountain looming ahead. This is Herðubreið, for centuries believed unclimbable because of its steep surrounding slopes of treacherous scree, until a German and an Icelander finally conquered it together in 1908. The greenery and vegetation here, fed by freshwater streams, come as something of a relief after all those barren miles of lava desert.

✚ 12B ✉ On Route F88; access strictly limited to July and August, be prepared for extreme weather conditions ❙❙ None ✋ Free

BLÖNDUÓS

This settlement on Route 1 is scattered on the flat green land around the mouth of the River Blanda and makes a good touring base. The town itself is unremarkable but boasts a unique and fascinating **textile museum** and a squat modern church of brown concrete, shaped like a volcanic crater and famous for its accoustics. There are salmon in the river and a rocky island called Hrútey, accessed by a bridge from the north bank, which is great for birdwatching. The Skagi peninsula stretches northward, luring you on with a promise of good birdwatching and seal-spotting.

To the south of the town, don't miss the solitary stone-built church of Þingeyrar (Thingeyrar) which marks a wealthy monastic site that was once central to the transcription of both the Bible and the Sagas; it has a fascinating interior with a star-painted ceiling and an unusual (English) altarpiece. Stand with your back to it and you'll find figures watching you from the gallery.

✠ 7D ✉ 145km (90 miles) west of Akureyri ⦙⦙ Various (£–££)
ℹ By the campsite ☎ 452 4520 ⓘ Jun–Aug 8am–9pm

Heimilisiðnaðarsafnið (Textile Museum)

✉ Árbraut 29, Blönduós ☎ 452 4067; www.simnet.is/textile 🕐 Jun–Sep daily 10–5 ✋ Inexpensive

BORGAFJÖRÐUR EYSTRI (BAKKAGERÐI)

For a town with two names, this is not a big one but is beautifully set on a broad bay, with a green valley behind and the dramatic mountain of Dyrfjöll (1,136m/3,726ft) beyond. With such a fine location, it's no surprise to know that the elves live around here in goodly numbers, notably inhabiting the small mound-with-a-view, Álfaborg. Look out for semi-precious stones at your feet – you can see examples in the **Álfasteinn** museum and shop. Iceland's famous landscape painter Jóhannes S Kjarval was raised near by at Geitavík, and you'll recognize the backdrop in his altarpiece in the church with Christ standing on Álfaborg.

www.borgafjordureystri.is

✚ 15C ✉ 336km (208 miles) east of Akureyri, on Route 94

Álfasteinn

☎ 470 2000; www.alfasteinn.is 🕐 Jun–Aug daily 10–6; Sep–May Mon–Fri 10–12 and 1–5 ✋ Free

DALVÍK

Looking at this busy fishing town today there's nothing to show that it was almost destroyed by a massive earthquake in 1934. It's beautifully set near the mouth of Eyjafjörður, with mountains behind and a view of the large island of Hrísey across the water. It's worth the short ferry ride to enjoy the peace and quiet of the nature reserve here. Hrísey's other claim to fame is as a quarantine island for livestock and pets coming into Iceland.

The **folk museum** in Dalvík has displays dedicated to local giant Jóhann Pétursson, who grew to 2.34m (7.7ft) high and became a Hollywood film star. Behind the town you can explore the interesting wetlands of Svarfaðardalur; a good leaflet, available locally, lists the marsh plants here and details of several walks. To the north, the precipitous road leads on to Ólafsfjörður; the silver ship memorial overlooking the fjord is to a local boat-builder, Eyvindur Jónsson, who died in 1746.

✚ 10E ✉ On Route 82, 44km (27 miles) north of Akureyri 🍴 Brekka Restaurant on Hrísey serves excellent Galloway beef, as well as lighter snacks ☎ 466 1751 ⛴ Scheduled ferry to Hrísey and Grímsey 🚩 Whale-watching tours ☎ 466 3355

Hvoll (Folk Museum)

✉ Karlsrauðatorg ☎ 466 1497 🕓 Jun–Aug daily 11–6 and on request ✋ Inexpensive

GOÐAFOSS

Travelling along the road from Akureyri to Mývatn you'll see what looks like a cloud of smoke over to your right, as though someone were burning off the heather. This is spray from the mighty horseshoe falls of Goðafoss; you can park at the petrol station-cum-store at Fosshóll, cross the deep gorge of the River

Skjálfandafljót and follow the well-worn path to view this beautiful waterfall. They're called the 'falls of the gods' after an incident in AD1000, when the Lawspeaker at the Alþing (parliament) decided in favour of the country becoming Christian and duly threw all his pagan idols in the water on his way home. This is a good place to hunt for wild flowers in the heath – look out for the delicate white flowers of mountain avens.

✚ 11D ✉ Off Route 1 ✋ Free 🍴 Coffee and snacks (£–££) at Fosshóll, also some accommodation ☎ 464 3108 🚌 All the tour buses stop here

GRÍMSEY

Contrary to popular expectation, most of Iceland lies south of the Arctic Circle, but this windswept island some 40km (25 miles) off shore is the exception, straddling the line at its northern tip. On a still, pink summer's evening, when the sun never quite sets on the horizon and the Arctic terns swoop overhead, it can seem a romantic spot, but the rest of the time there's not much to recommend it. The obligatory fingerpost which marks the circle line is a 25-minute walk up from the harbour, and offers the best photo-opportunity. To the north the razorbills, puffins and kittiwakes that once formed an important part of the island's economy nest noisily on the cliffs.

➕ 10F ✉ 41km (25 miles) north of mainland 🍴 Veitinghúsið Krian, summer and weekends only (£–££) ☎ 467 3112 ⛴ Regular ferry from Dalvík, and excursion boat ☎ 466 144 ✈ Flights from Akureyri with Air Iceland ☎ 460 7000

HÓLAR

Waymarked footpaths lead you around this attractive corner of the Haltadalur Valley. The first ever translation of the Bible in Icelandic was printed at Hólar in 1584. Until 1798 it was the seat of the northern bishopric, and the present cathedral is the fifth to be built here. It's worth a look in for the unusual chunky font of Greenland stone and the wonderfully vivid three-dimensional altarpiece, presented by Jón Arason, last Catholic bishop of Iceland, who served here from 1524–1550. After his execution at Skálholt (➤ 104–106) his body was brought here and buried under the separate belltower.

www.holar.is

➕ 9D ✉ On Route 767, 100km (62 miles) east of Blönduós 🕪 Church open daily 🍴 Summer snack bar in school building ✋ Free ❓ Guided tours of the church available 9–5 ℹ Old school building ☎ 455 6333/455 6300

HÚSAVÍK

Whale-watching has become one of Iceland's most popular tourist activities and Húsavík, a pleasant fishing town on the western shore of the rolling Tjörnes peninsula, is deservedly its capital. Spotting success rates are higher here than anywhere else – you're more or less guaranteed a sighting of the small minke whales, and there's a good chance you'll see the nobbly snouts and classic tail-flukes of humpback whales here too.

If the conditions are right, you may even be lucky enough to spot fin, sei and killer whales (orcas). Take binoculars and sun-glasses with you – the glare from the surface of the sea as you scour it for telltale puffs of whale-spout can be tiring. Don't miss a visit to the **Whale Centre** for a better understanding of these great sea-creatures – there are whole skeletons to wonder at, a touch table (try the shark skin!) and lots of fascinating information about the whales and dolphins found around Iceland. Iceland's famous **Phallological Museum** is a collection of some 150 preserved animal penises and other items, relocated here from Reykjavík in 2005, and offers a different sort of exhibition for a wet afternoon.

✚ 11E ✉ On Route 85, 91km (56 miles) northeast of Akureyri 🍴 Choice of places (£–£££) 🚢 Whale-watching tours from traditional wooden fishing boats, may be combined with puffin-watching on Lundey island ☎ 464 1500; www.gentlegiants.is ❓ For an introduction to the high-tech world of fish processing,the Whale Centre can arrange a tour of the local freezing plant
🛈 Garðarsbraut ☎ 464 4300

Hvalamiðstöðin (Whale Centre)
✉ Hafnarstétt ☎ 464 2520; www.icewhale.is 🕐 Flexible opening daily, May to mid-Sep 10–5; Jun–Aug 9–9 ✋ Inexpensive

Phallological Museum
✉ Hedinsbraut 3a ☎ 561 6663; www.phallus.is 🕐 Mid-May to mid-Sep daily 12–6 ✋ Inexpensive

a drive From Husavík to Mývatn

Start from Husavík and take Route 85 north up the coast.

Enjoy the views west to the cake-shaped island of Lundey, teeming with puffins through summer, and even of Grímsey on a clear day. After 4km (2.5 miles), the roadside monument is to poet Einar Benediktson.

Continue for 9km (6 miles) and turn into Hallbjarnastaðir to see the fossil museum. Retrace your route and after 3km (2 miles) turn right to Tjörneshöfn. The road to the harbour is steep and muddy – walk down if in doubt.

This is the best place to see the lines of compressed fossil shells in the cliffs.

Return to Húsavík, and stay on Route 85 towards Akureyri, crossing a big lava field covered with birch trees. After 39km (24 miles) turn left onto Route 845 for Laxárvirkjun.

This soon brings you to the pretty gabled farmhouse museum of Grenjaðarstaður; there's an ancient runic gravestone in the churchyard.

Return to Route 85 and turn left, to Laugar. At the junction with Route 1 turn left for Mývatn. Keep on Route 1 around the southern shore of the lake.

Lunch at the Hótel Gígur and stroll through green mounds scattered with periwinkles, or go on to Höfði for a picnic and walk through the birchwoods. Look out for whooper swans, tufted ducks, widgeon and Barrow's goldeneye on the lake, and listen for the drumming of snipe.

Continue to Reykjahlíð, and keep right on Route 1 for the sulphurous geothermal area of Námafjall, and Krafla power station 7km (4 miles) further on. Return to Reykjahlíð and bear right on Route 86 to return across the high moors to Húsavík.

Distance 195km (121 miles) **Time** All day, with stops for exploration
Start/end point Húsavík ✚ 11E
Lunch Hótel Gígur (££–£££) ✉ near Reykjalíð ☎ 464 4455;
www.keahotels.is
Fossil Museum ✉ Hallbjarnastaðir ☎ 464 1968 ◑ Jun–Aug
10–6 **Grenjaðarstaður Folk Museum** ☎ 464 3688; www.hus.mus
◑ Jun–Aug daily 10–6

JÖKULSÁRGLJÚFUR
See pages 42–43.

KJÖLUR

The high road through the interior known as Kjalvegur follows an old route between north and south which has been used since earliest times. Kjölur is the bare valley at the mid-point sandwiched between the Langjökull and Hofsjökull glaciers. To the north, the road passes through high boggy country towards Blöndurdalur; to the south the landscape is black and volcanic, stained with minerals and steaming areas of mud and sulphur. It feels cold here – there's a summer ski centre to the southeast on the flanks of Kerlingarfjöll. However, Kjölur holds a surprise – the geothermal oasis of Hveravellir, with hot springs of clear water, alpine flowers, a touring hut and campsite – and a weather station that is cut off from the world for most of the year. You can drive this route in a day in summer if the conditions are good ; in winter it's for the off-roaders.

✚ 21L ✉ Route F35 runs between Gullfoss and Blöndudalur; www.hveravellir.is 🍴 None 🚌 Scheduled summer buses take this route between Reykjavík and Akureyri; www.sba.is

MÝVATN
See pages 46–47.

SAURBÆR

The lovely sunny valley to the south of Akureyri is worth exploring for its four quite different churches, each found on a farm. You can loop up the west side of the valley on the 821 to Saurbær and return on

the opposite side (about 55km/34 miles). At Grund there is a large exotic-looking affair, with a red-painted onion dome and turrets, dating from 1905. The church at Saurbær is a more cosy traditional structure of timber and turf with a bell over the front door. It's from 1858 and marks the spot of a much older convent. On the return trip, the pretty white church at Möðruvellir has a strange wooden cage in the churchyard, a bell gate from 1781. The fourth church of interest is Munkaþverá (Munkathverá), on a former monastic site and more typical of the old Lutheran churches. The memorial beside it is to Jón Arason, last Catholic bishop of Iceland, who was born near by.

✠ 10C ✉ Saurbær is 27km (17 miles) south of Akureyri ✋ Free
❓ Ask locally for keys if locked

SIGLUFJÖRÐUR

This quiet little town on the northern coast, hemmed in by steep mountains and for years accessible only by sea, played a key role in the rapid growth of the Icelandic economy in the last century. For this was a herring boom town, alive with thousands of migratory workers throughout the season, its sheltered fjord packed with fishing boats. In 1916 alone 200,000 barrels of salted herring were exported from here, and at the height of the boom in the 1940s the town held 23 salting stations and 5 processing factories. Overfishing led to a crash of herring stocks in the 1960s and Siglufjörður's heyday came to an

end. It's a story well-told in photographs, film and memorabilia at the **museum** in the old herring station of Roaldsbrakki. On summer weekends it's brought to life again with the 'herring show' – a funny, lively dramatization of fishery days. Although it's in Icelandic you'll understand what's going on and can join in the dancing at the end.

www.siglo.is

✚ 9E ✉ Route 76, 192km (119 miles) northwest of Akureyri

ℹ In the Herring Era Museum

Síldarminjasafnið (Herring Era Museum)

☎ 467 1604 ✉ Snorragata ◷ Jun–Aug daily 10–6; spring and autumn 1–5

✋ Inexpensive ❓ Herring show Jul–Aug, weekends 3pm

VOPNAFJÖRÐUR

It's rumoured that Father Christmas lives to the south of this remote East Fjords town in the hill known as Smjörfjöll (butter mountain) – he probably comes here for the excellent fishing on the Selá and other local rivers. You'll climb the breathtaking hairpin bends on this mountain if you're travelling on the 917, and the views from the top are worth it. The settlement itself was once an important trading post but now concentrates on fisheries, with a harbour conveniently sheltered by low green islands. Route 85 brings you over some dreary high moors, but around the mountain of Bustarfell the views get more interesting and there's a charming old turf-clad **folk museum** there.

www.vopnafjardarhreppur.is

✚ 14D ✉ 233km (144 miles) east of Akureyri

ℹ Kaupvangur ☎ 473 1313 🕐 Summer only

Minjasafnið að Bustarfelli (Bustarfell Folk Museum)

✉ Bustarfell ☎ 473 1466 🕐 Mid-Jun to mid-Sep daily 10–6

🎫 Inexpensive 🍴 Café

HOTELS

AKUREYRI
Hótel KEA-Harpa (££–£££)

A very pleasant modern hotel at the foot of the steps to the cathdral, and in the heart of the old town. All rooms have private shower, TV and mini-bar, and there's an impressive restaurant.
✉ Hafnarstræti 87–89 ☎ 460 2000; www.keahotels.is ✪ All year

Staðarskáli (££)

Placed conveniently beside Route 1, this low-built, white-painted hotel offers good modern facilities, a restaurant, bicycles for hire,fishing, and the unusual option of goose hunting in autumn.
✉ Stadur, Hrútafjördur ☎ 451 1150; www.stadarskali.is ✪ All year

HÚSAVÍK
Fosshótel Husavík (££–£££)

What the décor may lack in modernity is more than made up for by the warm welcome you'll receive here – it's the friendliest hotel in Iceland, and with a great restaurant too. It's tucked up behind the Norwegian church, so central but quiet.
✉ Ketilsbraut 22 ☎ 464 1220 ✪ All year

LAUGAR
Fosshótel Laugar (£–££)

Comfortable summertime accommodation to the west of Mývatn. Facilities include a restaurant, bar and indoor swimming pool.
✉ Laugar ☎ 464 6300; www.fosshotel.is ✪ Jun–Aug

MIÐFJÖRÐUR
Brekkulækur (£–££)

Comfortable bed and breakfast accommodation (dinner on request) on a horse ranch, in a peaceful location in a broad green valley, handy for exploring the north coast. Specializes in guided trekking, both long- and short-distance, but also wildlife and hiking tours.
✉ Hvammstangi ☎ 451 2938 ✪ All year, including Christmas, but advance booking required Sep–May

MÝVATN
Sel-hótel Mývatn (££–£££)
A modern and comfortable hotel on Route 1, in a quiet area to the south of Reykjalíð, overlooking the lake.

✉ Skútustaðir ☎ 464 4164; www.myvatn.is ☀ Summer only

Vogarfarm Guesthouse (££)
This guesthouse beside the lake, just south of Reykjahlid, has comfortable accommodation in 20 rooms in low, modern timber-built blocks. The accommodation is part of a working dairy farm, where you can watch the cows being milked from the comfort of the café (7am and 5.30pm, summer only), and even try the job yourself.

✉ Vogar 1, Myvatn ☎ 464 4303 ☀ All year

RESTAURANTS

AKUREYRI
Bautinn (£–££)
This cheerful, no-frills restaurant occupies a great spot on the corner opposite the big book shop Bókval, with a conservatory dining room overlooking the main street. The house speciality is an excellent hamburger and chips, but you could try pasta with ham and mushrooms, or grilled salmon if you prefer. An Akureyri institution.

✉ Hafnarstræti 92 ☎ 462 1818 ☀ Lunch and dinner

Bláa Kannan (£)
Occupying one half of the magnificent old turreted building on Hafnarstræti, opposite Bókval bookstore and handy for downtown shopping. Inside, the stylish café has something of a French air, with lots of pale wood, chandeliers and modern art on the walls. There's a great selection of cakes to consume with your coffee as well as quiches and sandwiches, ideal for a light lunch. A no-smoking establishment.

✉ Hafnarstræti 96 ☎ 461 4600 ☀ Breakfast, lunch and dinner

Café Karólína (£–££)

Trendy café-cum-restaurant in Akureyri's stylish 'art' street, opposite the gallery of modern art.

✉ Kaupvangsstræti 23 ☎ 461 2755 🕐 Lunch and dinner

Fiðlarinn (££–£££)

Beautifully appointed and romantically lit modern restaurant overlooking the harbour area of Akureyri, with a wine bar in the lounge next door. International cuisine and an extensive wine list.

✉ Skipagata 14 ☎ 462 7100; www.fidlarinn.is 🕐 Lunch and dinner

Greifinn (£)

Children are welcome at this large bronze-coloured restaurant near the town centre, a favourite with local families. You can get anything from burgers and Tex-Mex to sophisticated Italian-Icelandic fusion: try salted cod glazed with basil pesto, served with a cheese rissotto, garlic roasted vegetables and a tomato herb sauce.

✉ Glerárgata 20 ☎ 460 1600; www.greifinn.is

HÚSAVÍK
Gamli Baukur (£–££)

In a modern timber building right on the harbour front, this lively restaurant is well placed for summer trade, spilling out onto the balcony on fine nights. Inside the woodwork is nautical and appealing, with old photos of Húsavík fishing boats. You can have anything from a snack of a bacon and cheese sandwich and chips or perhaps deep-fried prawns with a sweet and sour sauce; or splash out and try the tenderloin of lamb with ginger sauce. Daily specials, a children's menu and a good wine list.

✉ On the harbour ☎ 464 2442; www.gamlibaukur.is 🕐 May–Sep lunch and dinner

ENTERTAINMENT

Akureyri, Iceland's second city, is busy building up its own nightlife, though it can't compete with the capital.

CINEMAS

✉ Borgarbíó, Hólabraut 12, Akureyri ☎ 462 3500
✉ Nýja-Bíó, Ráðhústorgi 8, Akureyri ☎ 461 4666

NIGHTLIFE

Graeni Hatturinn

Extensive bar below the Blaa Kannan café, popular with all ages. Entrance via the café or from the side.
✉ Hafnarstræti 96, Akureyri ☎ 461 4646

Kaffi Akureyri

Evening bar, with live music at weekends, popular with younger crowd. Café by day.
✉ Strandgata 7, Akureyri ☎ 461 3999

Sjallinn

Lively pub and nightclub, with live bands at weekends. Great atmosphere. Over 18s.
✉ Geislagata 14, Akureyri ☎ 462 2770

THEATRE

Leikfélag Akureyrar

The only professional company outside Reykjavík, in historic theatre building.
✉ Hafnarstræti 57, Akureyri ☎ 460 0200; www.leikfelag.is

Listasumar

Organizes summer arts programmes of concerts, jazz and cultural events.
✉ Kaupvangsstræti 23, Akureyri ☎ 466 2609; www.akureyri.is

The South and Southeast

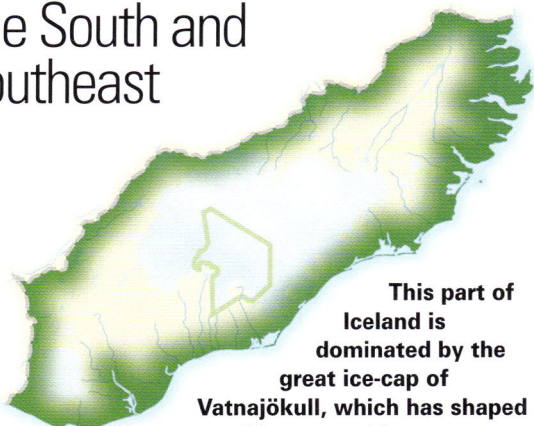

This part of Iceland is dominated by the great ice-cap of Vatnajökull, which has shaped everything around it.

Tongues of glacier ooze down between the mountains, and floodwaters have produced the vast desolate gravel and sand expanses (sandur) of Mýrdalssandur and Skeiðarársandur. The coastal lagoons around Höfn teem with migratory birds in spring and autumn, and after the steep fjords of the eastern coastline, the more expansive landscape of Fljótsdalur is welcome relief.

What to See in the South and Southeast

BREIÐDALSVÍK

An unexceptional village of low modern houses (winter gales in 2000 blew one of the last wooden houses to smithereens), Breiðdalsvík is nevertheless magnificent in its surroundings, with colourful rhyolite mountains tipped up to 1,200m (3,963ft) high behind, and lots of little bays popular with seals and eider ducks in front. The gradually retreating sea has left big gravel beds in the middle of the wide valley and so it's not surprising that early settlers, making their first landfalls here, chose to stay up the road at Snæhvammur– burial artefacts 1,000 years old were discovered here (now in the National Museum, Reykyavík). In 1942 a German aircraft attacked the village along with the spectacular lighthouse at Kambanes.

www.breiddalshreppur.is

✚ 15A ✉ 82km (51 miles) southeast of Egilsstaðir ▯ Café Margret
☎ 475 6625 🚤 Wildlife boat tours of islands in the area to see birds, seals and whales ☎ 864 0246/853 6946
ℹ District Office ☎ 475 6660

DJÚPIVOGUR

The houses of Djúpivogur perch among the rocks around the harbour on this rugged peninsula, with views out to the skerries around the low island of Papey. It seems incredible today that the village should have been a target for North African pirates in 1627. Roman coins were discovered to the west, prompting speculation that

the Romans also made it here, but it's now thought more likely that they were part of some Viking's plunder from Britain. The old **Langabúð** warehouse has an extraordinary museum of heads carved by local sculptor Ríkarður Jónsson (1888–1977), and a coffee shop. The area is famous for its zeolites – round stones which crack open to reveal beautiful crystals. Take a half-day boat trip to Papey, deserted now, but still with a tiny wooden church and lots of sea birds – the name suggests that its first settlers were Irish monks, probably scared off by Norse newcomers. The steep mountain ridge behind the town is Búlandstindur.

✚ 28L ✉ 146km (91 miles) south of Egilsstaðir ⛴ Cruises to Papey May–Sep ☎ 478 8183

Langabúð

☎ 478 8220 🕑 Jun–Aug daily 10–6 🍽 Pleasant summer café at Langabúð 🖐 Inexpensive

DYRHÓLAEY

This sheer headland jutting out some 120m (394ft) above the sea is a wildlife sanctuary and the southernmost point of mainland Iceland. It is reached via a causeway through hoodoos and a steep track up to the lighthouse. At its narrowest point the rock forms a natural arch over the water, big enough for tourist craft to sail through comfortably. A black sandy beach and another headland with picturesque pointed rock stacks at the end separate Dyrhólaey from the village of Vík, which has the unfortunate claim to be wetter than anywhere else in the country; more happily, it's the access point for the magnificent Mýrdalsjökull glacier.

www.dyrholaey.com

✚ 22G ✉ On route 218, 5km (3 miles) off Route 1 🕐 Open access, except at height of sea bird breeding season ⛴ Amphibious boat tours around Dyrhólaey ☎ 487 8500 ℹ Brydebúð, Víkurbraut 28, Vík ☎ 487 1395

EGILSSTAÐIR

Egilsstaðir lies about as far away from Reykjavík as you can get without leaving the ring road. It's a growing holiday town, lively with its own importance. The town's attractions include an open-

air market and the local history museum for East Iceland, but its chief interest for visitors (apart from its excellent sunshine record) is its setting on the River Lagarfljót. This flows down from the glacier of Vatnajökull, broadening to the south of town into the long, milky-blue lake of Lögurinn, which comes complete with its own shape-changing monster, the Lagarfljótsormurinn, and a forest at Hallormsstaður (▶ 148). There's lots to do here if you're feeling active, including reindeer hunting, as well as the more usual hiking, cycling, horse-back riding, skiing and trout fishing, and visits to the massive new Kárahnjúkar hydroelectric dam.

www.egilsstadir.is

✚ 15C ✉ Route 1, 698km (433 miles) east of Reykjavík 🚌 Scheduled coach service daily from Reykjavík and Akureyri 🍴 Range of cafés ❓ Summer cruises on the lake to Atlavík, Tue–Sun ☎ 471 2900. Also trips to Snæfell (▶ 154) ℹ Kaupvangur 10, by campsite ☎ 471 2320

HALLORMSSTAÐUR

It is believed that Iceland was once covered in trees, and reafforestation to prevent soil erosion is a major concern today. This is the largest forestry plantation in the country, covering some 740sq km (286 sq miles), and it provides a pleasant recreation area with walking trails and horse riding as well as a lovely campsite on the sandy lake shore at Atlavík. The tallest tree on the site is a Russian larch, planted in 1938 in memory of a forester.

🞧 14B ✉ On eastern shore of lake Lögurinn, on Route 931 ☎ 471 1774 (Atlavík campsite) ✋ Open access 🍴 Restaurant at Skriðuklauster museum (£–££), summer only 🛈 Easy access from Egilsstaðir

HÖFN

Try saying 'hup'n' while breathing in sharply, and you'll be somewhere near the correct pronunciation of this harbour town. Protected from the sea by two narrow spits of land, the town is beautifully set between two lagoons in a green oasis at the foot of sweeping mountains. For years it could only be reached by road from the north, but completion of the ring road in 1974 ended its isolation. Today Höfn's a convenient centre for exploring Vatnajökull and Jökulsárlón. The town has a Glacier Exhibition Centre on Hafnarbraut. It's well worth exploring the magnificent moss-covered valleys to the east, and the Lónsvík shore, teeming with eiders, swans and wild geese.

🞧 27K ✉ On route 1, 459km (285 miles) east of Reykjavík 🍴 Range of cafés and restaurants (£–£££) 🛈 Hátíð á Höfn (Lobster Festival) in early July with music, dance, competitions and feasting. Glacier Exhibition Centre: www.is-land.is

🛈 Litlabrú 2 ☎ 478 1500

JÖKULSÁRLÓN

See pages 44–45.

KIRKJUBÆJARKLAUSTUR

According to *Landnámabók* this area was first settled by Irish monks. Benedictine nuns occupied the site until 1550, and they are remembered in local place-names, such as the large outcrop of rock to the southwest called Systrastapi (Sisters' Rock). A natural feature called Kirkjugólf can be seen just off the junction with Route 203, towards Geirland – the smoothed tops of perfectly interlocking basalt rock columns, it looks like the tiled floor of a church (or a municipal pavement). The settlement lies in the shadow of the petrified lava-flow from the appallingly destructive volcano Laki; in 1783 the local hellfire preacher Jón Steingrímsson halted the lava just outside the village with his prayers. Summer tours from here can take you up the F206 to see the spectacular Lakakígar crater row.

www.klaustur.is

✚ 23H ✉ Route 1, 258km (160 miles) east of Reykjavík 🍴 Systrakaffi for tasty soup, fish and hamburgers (££)

ℹ Klausturvellir 10 ☎ 487 4840/487 4620

LANDMANNALAUGAR

Described as one of Iceland's 'natural jewels', this is certainly one of the most extensive and beautiful geothermal landscapes you'll see, surrounded by multi-coloured rhyolite mountains. Brennisteinsalda is just one of the highlights, streaked red, blue-grey and yellow, with all the colours in between and green moss for good measure. The combination of natural hot steam and cold fresh spring water makes the bathing pools just the right temperature. Don't hurry your visit, allowing at least a couple of days to explore the area – it's a long way from anywhere else and there's so much to discover – but note that accommodation is limited, and it gets very busy in summer.

✚ 22J ✉ On Route F208, 100km (62 miles) north of Route 1 🍴 Nearest coffee stop and petrol is Hrauneyjafosstöð, at junction of F208 and F26

❓ 4WD essential, and note the roads may be closed at short notice even in summer because of flooding

REYÐARFJÖRÐUR

The large number of recycled Nissen huts around Reyðarfjörður rather give the game away – there was an Allied base here during World War II. Lying midway between Europe and North America, Iceland played an important role as a strategic airbase for the Allies, and hundreds of soldiers were drafted in to defend it from possible German attack. You can discover more about this period at the **Wartime Museum** in the town. It's normally a quiet fishing town, on the sunny side of the biggest of the East Fjords, with a pleasing mix of old and new houses. It's on the road to Eskifjörður, and reached via a sweeping mountain pass and 6km (4-mile) tunnel from Egilsstaðir.

✚ 15B ✉ On Route 92, 34km (21 miles) south of Egilsstaðir

Stríðsárasafnið (Wartime Museum)

✉ Spítalakamp, V/Hæðagerði ☎ 470 9095 ◷ Jun–Aug daily 1–6
✋ Inexpensive

SEYÐISFJÖRÐUR

Old wooden Norwegian-style houses and a pretty blue-painted church make this one of the loveliest coastal towns in Iceland. It's set at the head of a narrow fjord, surrounded by steep mountains, and

it declined into its current genteel state after the herring boom. Artist Nina Tryggvadóttir was born in one of the merchants' houses on the central 'Ridge' in 1913. The church is particularly attractive inside and so well worth a look – if locked, knock at a neighbouring house for the key. The town has been the victim of avalanches and landslips over the years, and the twisted girder 'sculpture' at the town's northern entrance is evidence of the destruction caused by the last. You may spot rare harlequin ducks on the river behind the town.

www.seydisfjordur.is

✚ 15C ✉ 292km (181km) east of Akureyri, on Route 93 🍴 Hótel Seyðisfjörður, Austurvegur 3 ☎ 472 1460, or Skaftafell Cultural Centre, at Austurvegur 42 ☎ 4271632 ⛴ Weekly ferry *Norræna* sails to Faroes, Shetland, Norway and Denmark; May–Sep Thu; Oct–Apr Tue ☎ 472 1111 🛈 Ferry Pier ☎ 472 1551

SKAFTAFELL
See pages 48–49.

SKÓGAR

Don't miss this folk museum, tucked under the hills north of the ring road, near the southern point of the country. It's an outstanding and entertaining collection, started by curator Thórður Tómason when he was 14, with everything from Viking buttons to Iceland's first radio set (imported from Germany). There's a fully rigged fishing boat, the centrepiece of a fascinating fisheries and whaling exhibition, as well as historic costumes, embroidery, carved bedboards and all sorts of other domestic items, including rams' condoms, moulds for horn spoons and a lethally weighted mousetrap. Outside you can explore old turf-clad farmhouses, a school and a beautiful wooden church. If you're lucky, the curator himself will be on hand to show you around and play the harmoniums for you – be prepared to sing along. The 60m (228ft) waterfall at Skógar is also worth a look.

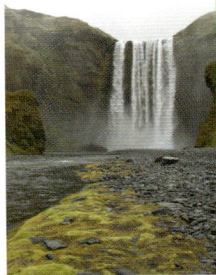

www.skogasafn.is

✚ 21G ✉ 154km (95 miles) east of Reykjavík ☎ 487 8845 🕔 Jun–Aug daily 9–6.30; Sep–May daily 10–5 ✋ Inexpensive 🍴 Café in museum

SNÆFELL

This old, snow-capped volcano, 1,833m (6,012ft) high, lies to the northeast of Vatnajökull, in an area of the interior most accessible from Fljótsdalur, and even then only in summer and with 4WD. One of the principal reasons to visit, apart from the fabulous views, is the chance of seeing wild reindeer. They graze on the tundra-like moss, lichen and grass on the moors up here, and more alarmingly, the shoots of young trees. They were first introduced from Norway at the end of the 18th century to provide an extra source of food for people. Winters proved too harsh and the experiment was never very successful, but this stock have survived and there are now several thousand roaming the hillsides. In a cold spring or autumn, you may find them nearer the coast.

✚ 27L ✉ Access via F910 from Fljótsdalur

VATNAJÖKULL

Vatnajökull actually dates from a mini-Ice Age only 2,500 years ago. The biggest ice-cap in Europe (in fact, at over 8,000sq km/3,088 miles, bigger than all the others put together), it is a temperate glacier, inherently unstable, which makes life difficult and sometimes dangerous for

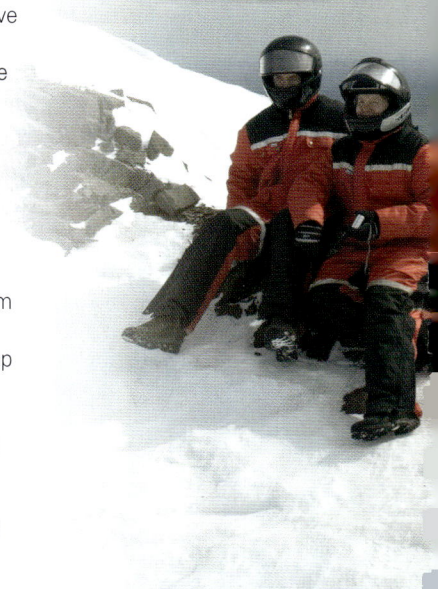

those who live around its edges. (Not that this stops visitors having a fine time exploring on skidoos.) It lies like a 1km-thick (0.6 mile) blanket, cold but not entirely frozen, smothering the top of several live volcanoes, and when they errupt – as Grímsvötn did in 1996 – the ice quickly melts. The meltwater gathers in under-ice lakes until it overflows in a massive *hlaup*, bringing quantities of mud, rock and icebergs sweeping down onto the plains, reshaping the landscape as it goes. Its glacier fingers spread along the southern coast of Iceland, most beautifully at Jökulsárlón (➤ 44–45).

✚ 25K ❓ Join a guided tour from Höfn (➤ 148) up to Skálafellsjökull for the best access on to the glacier – tours are by snow scooter or snow tractor

HOTELS

EGILSSTAÐIR
Gistihúsið Egilsstödum (£–££)
Beautiful old house overlooking the lake. Comfortable and friendly.
✉ Egilsstaðir ☎ 471 1114 🕐 All year

HÖFN
Árnanes (£–££)
Close to the local airport (not busy) are these five wooden houses, with a good restaurant on site.
✉ 781 Hornafjörður ☎ 478 1550; www/arnanes.is 🕐 All year

Hótel Höfn (££–£££)
Just on the edge of the town centre, with good views and its own top-notch pizzeria – and the fish and chips are good, too.
✉ Víkurbraut 24 ☎ 478 1240 🕐 All year

MÝRDALUR
Sólheimahjáleiga (£)
Simple bed and breakfast accommodation in an old farmhouse, with shared facilities and a great view from the kitchen window.
✉ Mýrdalur ☎ 467 1320 🕐 All year

RESTAURANTS

BREIÐDALSVÍK
Margret's Café (£–££)
This wooden chalet above the road has fabulous views over the inlet. A cosy interior, with lots of exposed wood and the aroma of freshly brewed speciality coffees. Accommodation also available.
✉ Heimaleiti, Breiddalsvík ☎ 475 6625 🕐 All year

Kaffi Hornið (£–££)
A light and airy, well-placed restaurant on the main road to the harbour. The menu has a bistro feel – there are grilled sandwiches, more substantial pasta dishes (such as creamy pasta with lobster, bread and salad) and good vegetarian choices, too.
✉ Hafnarbraut 42 ☎ 478 2600 🕐 Mon–Sat lunch and dinner

Index

Acknowledgements

The Automobile Association would like to thank the following photographers and companies for their assistance in the preparation of this book. Abbreviations for credits are as follows – (t) top; (b) bottom; (c) centre; (l) left; (r) right; (AA) AA World Travel Library

4l Blue Lagoon AA/J Tims; **4c** Ferry AA/J Tims; **4r** Myvatn Lake AA/J Tims; **5l** Sailing AA/J Tims; **5c** Hallgrimskirkja AA/J Tims; **6/7** Blue Lagoon AA/J Tims; **8/9** Skaftafell AA/J Tims; **10/11t** Þjoðmenning, Culture House AA/J Tims; **10c** Jökulsárlón AA/J Tims; **11c** Statue of Leifur Eiriksson by Alexander Calder AA/J Tims; **10/11b** Dimmuborgir AA/J Tims; **12/13t** Flatey Island AA/J Tims; **12/13c** Höfn AA/J Tims; **12b** Höfn AA/J Tims; **13cr** Sheep AA/J Tims; **13b** Restaurant sign AA/J Tims; **14t** Café Nielsen AA/J Tims; **14c** Liquor store sign AA/J Tims; **14b** Local beer AA/J Tims; **15** Reykjavik street scene AA/J Tims; **16** Myvatn Nature Baths AA/J Tims; **17t** Icelandic horses AA/J Tims; **17c** Skidoo AA/J Tims; **17b** Puffin AA/Ronnie Weir; **18/19** Ferry, Flatey Island AA/J Tims; **24** Vestmannaeyjar AA/J Tims; **25** Jeep AA/J Tims; **26c** Road signs AA/J Tims; **26b** Airport, Reykjavik AA/J Tims; **27t** Bus, Reykjavik AA/J Tims; **27c** Ferry, Flatey Island AA/J Tims; **27b** Taxi AA/J Tims; **28** ATM AA/J Tims; **32/33** Myvatn Lake AA/J Tims; **35** Blue Lagoon AA/J Tims; **36t, 36/37b, 37t** Flatey Island AA/J Tims; **38/39** Gullfoss AA/J Tims; **39br** Geysir, Strokkur (the Churn) AA/J Tims; **40l** View of Hallgrimskirkja AA/J Tims; **41t** Interior of Hallgrimskirkja AA/J Tims; **41b** Hallgrimskirkja AA/J Tims; **42/43t, 42b** Jökulsárgljúfur Ange/Alamy; **44/45, 45t** Jökulsárlón, glacial lagoon AA/J Tims; **45br** Amphibious vehicle AA/J Tims; **46b, 47br** Myvatn Lake AA/J Tims; **47t** Dimmuborgir AA/J Tims; **48bl, 49tr** Skaftafellsjökull finger of Vatnajökull glacier AA/J Tims; **48/49** Skaftafell, Svartifoss waterfall AA/J Tims; **50cl, 50/51b** Þingvellir AA/J Tims; **51tl** Þingvellir, site of the first Alþing marked by flagpole AA/J Tims; **52/53t, 52/53b** Vestmannaeyjar, Heimaey AA/J Tims; **54/55** Sailing, Reykjavik AA/J Tims; **56** Akureyri AA/J Tims; **57** Reykjavik, Austurvöllur AA/J Tims; **58** Hveragerði, cyclist AA/J Tims; **59** Skalafellsjökull glacier AA/J Tims; **61** Svartifoss waterfall AA/J Tims; **62, 63** Reykjavik Family Park and Zoo AA/J Tims; **64/65** Reykjavik, Kaffi Solon AA/J Tims; **66** Reykjavik, Laugavegur AA/J Tims; **67** Shop AA/J Tims; **68/69** View of Hallgrimskirkja AA/J Tims; **71** Arnarstapi AA/J Tims; **72/73** Reykjavik from Hallgrimskirkja AA/J Tims; **74** Árbæjarsafn AA/J Tims; **74/75b** Ásmundarsafn AA/J Tims; **76/77** Austurvöllur square AA/J Tims; **77br** Bernhöftstorfan, Government House AA/J Tims; **78bl, 78/79b** Höfn AA/J Tims; **80bl, 80/81** Laugardalur, AA/J Tims; **81c** Listasafn Íslands AA/J Tims; **82** Skólavörðustigur AA/J Tims; **84t** Einar Jónsson Sculpture Museum AA/J Tims; **84b, 85t** Öskjuhlíð, Architect Ingimundur Sveinsson, AA/J Tims; **85b** Öskjuhlíð, Saga Museum AA/J Tims; **86** Þjoðmenning, Melsted's Edda manuscript, 1765, Arnamagnaean Institute in Iceland/AA/J Tims; **87** Þjoðminjasafn Íslands, interior with traditional fishing boat AA/J Tims; **88t, 88b** Tjörnin AA/J Tims; **89** Viðey Island AA/J Tims; **90/91** Arnarstapi AA/J Tims; **91tr** Borgarnes AA/J Tims; **92bl, 93b** Hafnarfjörður, Fjörukráin AA/J Tims; **92/93t** Hafnarfjörður, harbour AA/J Tims; **94** Hafnir AA/J Tims; **96/97** Glacial stream north of Húsafell AA/J Tims; **98b** Hvalfjörður AA/J Tims; **99t** Reykholt, thermal pool AA/J Tims; **100t** Hvalfjörður AA/J Tims; **101tr** Hveragerði AA/J Tims; **101b** Hvolsvöllur, Saga Centre AA/J Tims; **102/103** Krýsuvík AA/J Tims; **104** Reykholt, thermal pool AA/J Tims; **105** Reykholt, new church AA/J Tims; **106/107** Stykkishólmur AA/J Tims; **108/109** Stykkishólmur AA/J Tims; **110** Þorsmörk Nordicphotos/Alamy; **117** Goðafoss waterfall AA/J Tims; **118/119** Akureyri AA/J Tims; **120** Akureyri, church AA/J Tims; **121** Minjasafn Akureyrar AA/J Tims; **122/123** Viti crater lake, Askja, Bernd Mellmann/Alamy; **124** Blönduós AA/J Tims; **126** Dalvik, ferry AA/J Tims; **127** Goðafoss waterfall AA/J Tims; **128** Hólar, Nyibær farm house built by Benedikt Vigfusson in 1860 AA/J Tims; **129** Hólar, church bell tower AA/J Tims; **130/131t** Húsavík Whale Centre AA/J Tims; **130b** Húsavík AA/J Tims; **132/133** Námafjall AA/J Tims; **134** Grund, church AA/J Tims; **135** Saurbær, church AA/J Tims; **136t, 136/137** Siglufjörður, Herring Museum AA/J Tims; **138** Vopnafjörður, Ragnar Th. Sigurosson; **143** Seyðisfjörður AA/J Tims; **144bl** Djúpivogur AA/J Tims; **145** Djúpivogur, Ragnar Th. Sigurosson; **146/147** Dyrhólaey AA/J Tims; **147tr** Egilsstaðir, Local History Museum AA/J Tims; **148bl** Höfn AA/J Tims; **149** Kirkjubæjarklaustur, Kirkjugólf AA/J Tims; **150/151t, 151b** Reyðarfjörður AA/J Tims; **152/153** Seyðisfjörður, church AA/J Tims; **153tr** Skógar, Folk Museum AA/J Tims; **153br** Skógafoss waterfall AA/J Tims; **154/155** Skalafellsjökull finger of Vatnajökull glacier AA/J Tims

Every effort has been made to trace the copyright holders, and we apologise in advance for any accidental errors. We would be happy to apply the corrections in the following edition of this publication.

Dear Reader

Your comments, opinions and recommendations are very important to us. Please help us to improve our travel guides by taking a few minutes to complete this simple questionnaire.

You do not need a stamp (unless posted outside the UK). If you do not want to cut this page from your guide, then photocopy it or write your answers on a plain sheet of paper.

Send to: **The Editor, AA World Travel Guides, FREEPOST SCE 4598, Basingstoke RG21 4GY.**

Your recommendations...

We always encourage readers' recommendations for restaurants, nightlife or shopping – if your recommendation is used in the next edition of the guide, we will send you a **FREE AA Guide** of your choice from this series. Please state below the establishment name, location and your reasons for recommending it.

_____

_____

_____

_____

_____

_____

Please send me **AA Guide** _____

About this guide...

Which title did you buy?

AA _____

Where did you buy it? _____

When? m m / y y

Why did you choose this guide? _____

_____

_____

_____

_____

Did this guide meet your expectations?

Exceeded ☐   Met all ☐   Met most ☐   Fell below ☐

Were there any aspects of this guide that you particularly liked? _____

_____

_____

_____

continued on next page...

Is there anything we could have done better? _____
_____
_____
_____

About you...
Name (*Mr/Mrs/Ms*) _____
Address _____
_____
_____ Postcode _____

Daytime tel nos _____
Email _____

Please only give us your mobile phone number or email if you wish to hear from us about
other products and services from the AA and partners by text or mms, or email.

Which age group are you in?
Under 25 ☐   25–34 ☐   35–44 ☐   45–54 ☐   55–64 ☐   65+ ☐

How many trips do you make a year?
Less than one ☐   One ☐   Two ☐   Three or more ☐

Are you an AA member? Yes ☐   No ☐

About your trip...
When did you book? m m / y y   When did you travel? m m / y y

How long did you stay? _____

Was it for business or leisure? _____

Did you buy any other travel guides for your trip? _____

If yes, which ones? _____
_____
_____

Thank you for taking the time to complete this questionnaire. Please send it to us as soon as
possible, and remember, you do not need a stamp (*unless posted outside the UK*).

| **AA** Travel Insurance call 0800 072 4168 or visit www.theAA.com |